The Briefcase Effect Praise

'Equal parts clarity, wisdom and warmth. *The Briefcase Effect* makes personal branding feel do-able, not daunting, with tools you can apply to your business and your everyday decisions. Vinisha has a way of turning big ideas into bite-sized metaphors you'll remember forever. This book is practical, powerful and deeply human. A must-read for building a brand (and a life) you actually love!'

FRANCES GOH, co-founder, One Roof

'I was not sure what to think when I picked up *The Briefcase Effect*, but found it to be an extremely interesting read. It outlined steps on what I should be looking into as an entrepreneur and ambitious female. The reflective questions were interesting but gave me a very different perspective on some of my decisions. It will be a book that I come back to again and again. Thank you, Vinisha!'

ALEXANDRA LARACH, founder, Visionary Events

'Personal branding isn't just about visibility – it's about impact. In the tech world, where voices can get lost in the noise, LinkedIn has been my playground for shaping narratives that matter. Reading *The Briefcase Effect* made me pause and rethink what I carry forward. Vinisha doesn't just talk about branding; she redefines it as a tool for connection, purpose and leadership. This book is a must-read for anyone, especially women who want to show up fully, own their story, and build a brand that actually reflects who they are.'

SINÉAD FITZGERALD, HealthTech Partnerships at Microsoft Asia and co-founder, Health Innovators Circle

'What makes *The Briefcase Effect* so brilliant is that it doesn't overwhelm you with a never-ending to-do list or yet another productivity hack. Instead, it offers something far more valuable: a mindset shift. This book teaches you how to live and lead from a place of authenticity. It gently guides you back to yourself – so that business, creativity and goal-setting stem from alignment rather than hustle.

Vinisha offers a blueprint for how to use your most precious and finite resource – your time – in a way that feels light, fun and fulfilling. It's not just a book about personal branding; it's about building a life that reflects who you truly are. A life where progress feels natural, not forced. Full of evergreen wisdom and practical, soul-stirring insights, *The Briefcase Effect* is a book you'll want to revisit again and again.'

ORSOLYA MÁRIA TÓTH-PÁL, founder, Debate Club and Suntied

'Reading *The Briefcase Effect* is like opening a handwritten letter from your future self. It's gentle, generous, and glowing with the grounded guidance that you didn't know you needed.'

PAZ PISARSKI, co-founder, The Community Collective

'This isn't a book about being "more polished". It's a book about being more you. By drawing on her lived experience and own success story, Vinisha has created a roadmap to clarity, confidence and alignment for anyone navigating change, reinvention and self-discovery. From this wisdom flows a personal brand that is not only genuinely, but truly effortless to express and build.'

LIZ VAN ZYL, startup ecosystem and community builder

'*The Briefcase Effect* is a must read for everyone – whether you're starting out in your career or you're a seasoned pro. It will help you unpack and connect to your truest "why" and guide you to aligned choices not just in work but in life. Such an enjoyable and practical read, like having an honest conversation with a friend – Vinisha has packaged up personal branding in such a way that makes it accessible to everyone. I only wish I had this sooner! I'm currently in a transition period in my career, and this blueprint has kept me grounded, clear-headed, and moving forward with purpose.'

MONIKA VEITH, founder, The MV edit

'*The Briefcase Effect* is more than a guide to personal branding – it's a call to authenticity. Vinisha blends heartfelt storytelling with practical wisdom, empowering readers to show up boldly and unapologetically. Her framework – rooted in self-awareness, purpose and connection – makes personal branding feel deeply human and actionable. This book is a must-read for anyone ready to align who they are with how they lead, live, and show up in the world.'

LAKUN AGRAWAL, Chief Financial Officer

'This is a refreshing and inspiring guide to integrating and improving personal brand. Written based on solid research and relevant refined personal experiences, and presented with beautiful candour, *The Briefcase Effect* is a worthwhile read. I wish I'd had access to this book sooner!'

RACHEL FERRIS, consultant and author

'*The Briefcase Effect* beautifully unravels the building blocks of life that make up the human experience and, ultimately, the "personal" in personal brand. It has the courage and emotional acumen to tackle the messy humanness of the person behind the career. A practical, thoughtful and articulate guide to achieving a satisfying work life and authentic personal brand.'

ADA YIN, healthtech founder

'As someone building a business, this book resonated deeply. *The Briefcase Effect* is a powerful book that will enable readers to understand themselves, build meaningful partnerships and be profound leaders.'

NEHA J, founder of Bindaas Bilinguals and writer

'This book is the guide to working out who you wanna be when you grow up. Vinisha generously shares her lessons and knowledge to wrap you in warmth while gently peppering you with the truths you always needed to hear. The world needs more Vinishas and this book is a fabulous stop gap.'

TEALA STEPHENS, angel investor and community builder

'Vinisha has rapidly built a public profile in the Startup sector and this book distills her learnings for those looking to understand the power of personal brand and how to shape their own in an authentic way.'

KALI NORMAN, community builder and conference curator

'In a crowded world of "same-same" personal-branding guides, Vinisha's wisdom cuts through the noise. Her focus on People, Purpose and Partnership will help every reader reclaim their essence and build meaningful connections with themselves and those around them.'

LAETITIA ANDRAC, author and co-founder, Understanding Zoe and Essential Shift

The Briefcase Effect beautifully balances vulnerability, self-compassion and energetic empowerment with a refreshingly practical approach to personal branding. As someone who once carried a leopard-print briefcase into a corporate world that didn't quite fit, this book resonated deeply. It's a powerful guide for anyone ready to lead, grow and build a business – or a life – that reflects who they really are.'

RAYLENE SYMONS, founder, Saltwater Digital

'This book landed with me in a way I didn't expect. I picked it up out of curiosity, but it quickly became exactly what I needed – not because I felt lost, but because it gave me space to reflect on the brand I've already built and whether it's the one I truly want. It made me pause, reset and feel more intentional about what I carry forward.'

JACQUI MOORE-MORONEY, founder and principal consultant, Moore Moroney Consulting

'Vinisha exploded into the Australian entrepreneurial ecosystem with her unique blend of authenticity, mastery and humour. This book is a window into how she quickly became a powerhouse for change.'

MIC BLACK, biotech founder

THE
BRIEFCASE
EFFECT

THE BRIEFCASE EFFECT

Your Personal Brand Action Plan:
For the Curious and the Courageous

VINISHA RATHOD

GRAMMAR
FACTORY
— EST© 2013 —

Published by Grammar Factory Publishing, an imprint of MacMillan
Company Limited.

Grammar Factory Publishing
MacMillan Company Limited
25 Telegram Mews, 39th Floor, Suite 3906
Toronto, Ontario, Canada
M5V 3Z1

www.grammarfactory.com

Rathod, Vinisha.
The Briefcase Effect: Your Personal Brand Action Plan:
For the Curious and the Courageous / Vinisha Rathod.

Paperback ISBN 978-1-998528-32-5
Hardcover ISBN 978-1-998528-34-9
eBook ISBN 978-1-998528-33-2

1. BUS012030 Business & Economics / Careers /
Career Advancement & Professional Development.
2. SEL021000 Self-Help / Motivational & Inspirational.
3. BUS109000 BUSINESS & ECONOMICS / Women in Business.

PRODUCTION CREDITS
Cover design by Designerbility
Interior layout design by Setareh Ashrafologhalai
Book production and editorial services by Grammar Factory Publishing

GRAMMAR FACTORY'S CARBON NEUTRAL PUBLISHING COMMITMENT
Grammar Factory Publishing is proud to be neutralising the carbon footprint of all printed copies of its authors' books printed by or ordered directly
through Grammar Factory or its affiliated companies through the purchase
of Gold Standard-Certified International Offsets.

I would love to acknowledge the Traditional Owners and innovators of this land, where I was inspired to create. Growing up in a home where books were so revered, I never imagined – not even in my wildest dreams – that we would be here. Becoming an author wasn't on the to-do list, and I am both honoured and delighted that you are spending your moments with me.

I dedicate this to all of you searching for clarity and navigating this world looking for a 'purpose' and to live a fulfilling life (spoiler: you don't need to have everything figured out).

To my mother, grandmothers and ancestors who challenge cultural constructs and broke cycles so we could thrive, thank you, your efforts will not go to waste.

To my father, who passed away when I was twenty-two, I dedicate this book to you, a man who pursued one of the greatest journeys known to the human race; the knowing of self. To my late grandfathers, who also passed too soon, thank you for being the curious ones who knew there had to be more. Your entrepreneurial spirit, courage and love for humanity run through my veins.

I miss you all so much. Thank you for always finding a way to be by my side. I hope I make you proud.

CONTENTS

Equal
Equal
Work
aussie angel
T-EDI Standards
GROUP
GROUP
DO THE
PICK CHERRIES NOT DATA
END GENDER-BASED
SOUTH BY SOUTHWEST
WTF FESTIVAL PASS
OVERNIGHT SUCCESS
Super Fan
TEAM HUMAN
Storm Chaser
JUICY INSIGHTS
DATA WOMEN
Talking Healthtech

PREFACE

SPENT MANY YEARS struggling to find my place in the world and at work. Many people called me a 'late bloomer' (maybe you can relate). I followed the rules in my corporate career: I kept my head down, waited for my managers to recognise my efforts, got promoted and continued the cycle. I often felt I was riding the merry-go-round at work and in my personal life. But I knew in my curious heart that there was more. There had to be more among all this craziness – an easier way for me to work with the world rather that constantly fighting to be in it.

Sometimes you stumble upon the answers to your questions unexpectedly, and this was very true as I entered into a completely new industry and chapter of my life. Little did I know that an ordinary bus ride would shape my life, my work and this book you are reading.

I was starting a new job and needed a new bag for my laptop, and there it was on a bus ride I took one day – a man holding a brown leather briefcase and half a litre of milk in the same hand. It was at that moment that I was flooded with memories of my father, who used to carry a briefcase to work. He had a black one. I miss him every day. He was diagnosed with cancer a couple of months after I graduated from university, and within four months one of the people closest to me was taken away. I was twenty-two, he was fifty. Watching someone you love dying in front of you – nothing prepares you for that.

Because of this, he never saw me succeed in business. The startup world is the closest parallel to the science fiction stories we grew up with. He would have found his place in it and been quietly proud to see me in mine. After years of feeling disconnected, I was searching for a sign that I was on the right track. I smiled, grateful for the sign I'd been searching for. My dad would have *loved* that man's briefcase.

It was in that moment on the bus that I knew a modern-day briefcase was going to be my new laptop bag; something that would embody Dad's spirit so he could be with me every step of the way. After searching store after store with my mum and almost giving up (it turns out briefcases aren't so popular nowadays), I finally found one. It wasn't long before the briefcase started gaining attention from my friends, colleagues and clients. I've brought it everywhere, from networking events to conferences and meetings, and no matter where I am it's always a topic of discussion.

Without realising it, my briefcase (and my dad's spirit) became a core part of my personal brand as a professional. And that was only the tip of the iceberg. As I learned more about my new industry and grew my confidence in my new role, the meaning behind the briefcase and the conversations it evoked became deeper. It always starts with the same question, 'Hey V, what's in the briefcase?' I've narrowed it down to three things:

1   Venture Capital Money,[1]

2   'Thoughts and prayers', and

3   Secrets to sustainably scaling your business.

If the first two items don't pique somebody's interest, the last one always does, and it's become a key part of my networking strategy to build new connections.

I quickly realised that my personal brand – my briefcase – had become a core part of my success and decided to lean into it. I built my brand based on what I love and who I am as my most authentic self; my bold fashion, colourful nails and big statement earrings represent my daring and creative, yet professional approach to business. And it earned me the endearing title of the 'Startup Fairy' within the Australian tech ecosystem.

I knew no one when I entered into the system three years ago, and now (in 2025) I am often called by the community to speak and share my thought leadership in authenticity, personal branding, diversity, glass ceilings and ending domestic violence.

The briefcase, my brand, has become my magic power for success and contentment in life – leaning into my authenticity had a ripple effect on how I put myself out into the world. For the first time in my life, I was able to integrate my personality into my work, and the Briefcase Effect only enhanced what happened next.

Because of my established brand in the market, the transition to my own business was easier. People already knew

---

1   Venture Capital means a corporation which provides money for fast-growth, high-risk tech companies, usually in exchange for shares.

who I was due to my presence both offline and online. I will reiterate that I was learning this on the fly. As we dive into this book, I will share why this has been a big game-changer for someone like me. I didn't really know how to navigate the working world, as it wasn't really shown to me. I didn't grow up in that environment and I lost my father as I was entering it properly, and so I didn't really have anyone to rely on after he passed.

What I wish I had known earlier in my journey is this: people buy people, and if you are going to build your own business, people want to know if they can trust you. Living in a digital-first society, we have both online and real-life personas, making authenticity and relatability even more important. With the Fourth Industrial Revolution of generative AI (artificial intelligence) already coming into force, it's important to understand your greatest strength when navigating the commercial world, and that's *you*; your essence. This is the Briefcase Effect.

This is the book I always wish I had when I was trying to figure out my life and career!

By the end of this book, you will know what your strong suit is, what your natural talent is, and how to harness it so you can live life on your terms and have fun while doing so. When you are intentional with your decisions, then peace, contentment and fun all follow.

You will be clear in how you want to spend your waking hours, and have less need to fill in the space with activities such as lavish holidays,[2] drugs, drinking, yoga retreats and other forms of escapism – imagine if what you want, how

---

2   Please understand that I enjoy travel and holidays; however, there is a significant difference between taking a holiday for relaxation and using travel as a means of escapism to avoid facing one's reality. We will touch on this later; escapism as avoidance versus healthy coping mechanisms.

you feel and what you do were all completely aligned? What if you no longer needed to pretend and you started to attract opportunities that you actually want to be part of?

If you are reading this and wondering if it's too late to start living life on your terms, please don't think that. I only started building my presence properly three years ago, and my life has changed completely! We will unpack the Briefcase Effect together so you can start to lead a career and a life you love.

INTRODUCTION
YOUR BRIEFCASE
MATTERS

People do not buy goods and services.
They buy relations, stories and magic.

SETH GODIN
entrepreneur, thought
leader, best-selling author

WROTE THIS BOOK as an everyday person who is looking to do her part to make the world a better place. I don't
have shiny accolades, fancy awards, tens of thousands
of followers or a picture-perfect path, but I am someone
who's lived the questions. Once upon a time, I wondered how
to show up for myself so consistently that it would ripple
through every part of my life. I used to be lost, unsettled,
and uncertain in everything I did, all the time. I am someone
who's made a mess, started over, and learned how to build
a life from the inside out.

You're probably wondering, 'Vinisha, how could personal branding possibly have such an impact on my life?'

Well, although this book is about how to build your personal brand, at its core it's about uncovering the best version of you, figuring out what you want, and getting so comfortable and cosy in your own skin that you can accomplish whatever you set your sights on, confidently and in your own style.

I am writing this today because after many years I have truly built a life where I don't need to run away, and I am so content and secure in myself that even if I had ten million dollars in my bank, I would still be doing the same work, caring about the same things and showing up the same way – completely aligned and fully present, not stuck in a loop of overthinking or worrying.

Imagine if the need to run away or escape the grind was no longer there – imagine that when you drink, take a holiday, take drugs, gamble or perform it is because you *want* to, not because you need to forget or run away. Can you imagine how different your life would be if that were the case? This is not to take away from having fun; it's about having fun, and living and building a career on your terms – a career that supports and is aligned with the life you want to lead.

I write this as someone who is by no means extravagant but deeply intentional in how I show up and live in all aspects of life, and if I can do it, I am telling you *anyone* can do it. You already have all the answers within yourself.

Why this book and why me?

If you've ever wondered whether your lived experience counts as expertise, this book is for you. The Briefcase Effect methodology is a three-year overnight success story. It all began when I shifted industries and entered the world of tech and creatives. I started working for a tech recruitment company, and the most common question people asked each other was (can you guess it?), 'What are you passionate about?'

From my observations, I found passion can be very fleeting. People often abandon good jobs once they lose interest in them; however, mastering a craft takes time. It takes discipline, and the more you persist, the better you become. If you apply that in a work context, that expertise earns your trust. People rely on you. And that directly impacts your opportunities – and your income.

So I started asking: *What professional muscle do you want to grow?*

That reframe – mastery over momentary excitement – was noticed. Startups invited me to mentor their teams. I found myself coaching people (often women) who were navigating redundancy, reinvention or identity shifts at work. I was helping them uncover skills they didn't know they had – and naming the value they already carried.

What began as conversations became a framework. That framework became part of my business. And that business became the Briefcase Effect.

It wasn't always this way. When I came back from overseas after several years – broke, grieving and invisible – no one handed me a map. So, I made one, just one, small step at a time. I realised how painfully invisible I'd been. I had no career fairy godmother. No inherited networks. No training in how to show up online. After months and months of job hunting, a friend helped me get a role in retail to get me back on my feet. I was a story untold, similar to many of us who didn't know that social media could be strategic, or that personal brand was more than followers, polished headshots and perfect bios.

I am far from the perfect person; however, if you saw what my life was three years ago compared to now, you'll see that I have completely shifted my personal and professional environment, which has had a significant impact on the trajectory of my life. I was finally welcomed, and when a little part of me was shared with the world, with the help of the Briefcase Effect, more and more parts started showing themselves. And people liked those authentic parts of me that were showing up. I was surprised. There are many ways my strong personal brand has helped me, and many ways yours can help you too.

Why not this book?

As technology becomes more central to how we live and work, building a personal brand is one of the most empowering things you can do to stay aligned and visible. We are constantly looking for ways to build trust, as we are all more cautious than we have ever been (and rightly so). People love to buy people and their stories, so it is important to stand out in a way that is very authentic to you, whether you're starting your own business, relaunching your career or starting a new chapter in life. Relationships are the heart of human experience, and how you show up in them (your personal brand) can play a big role in defining your life, especially if you don't already have established networks.

I have seen many people miss out on opportunities due to a lack of clarity or confidence, or because they haven't yet learned how to express their value clearly. These questions can help highlight where things feel off, and where you may want to explore more alignment.

- What are my most valuable skills?
- What do I stand for or deeply care about?
- Where should I focus my time and effort?
- How do I show up for my community? Do I even enjoy their company?
- What do I say yes or no to?

- What do I personally value?
- Where do I fit in this world?
- How do I cope when I am overwhelmed?

This book aims to help you bring the answers to these questions to light so you can understand your place in this world better, show up intentionally, and feel more harmony with who you are and what you do.

'The meaning of life is just be alive. It is so plain and so obvious and so simple. And yet, everybody rushes around in a great panic as if it were necessary to achieve something beyond themselves.'

ALAN WATTS

How to use this book

One of the greatest gifts you can give the world is choosing to become the best version of yourself. The belief that personal and professional lives are separate is outdated – today, they are deeply intertwined. This book is designed to help you build, own and drive your personal brand. It's about knowing when to push for change and when to let go. This is a practical guide. You can engage with it in multiple ways:

- **Option A**: Use it as a point of reference – something to learn from and use to spark great conversations at work or social gatherings.

- **Option B**: Follow it as a step-by-step guide to building your personal brand, as if we were working together in a one-on-one session, where I would sit with you to develop your brand and plan for success.

No matter which option you choose or how you decide to engage with this book, here are some tips to ensure you get the most out of it:

1 **Write it down**. Whether typing or writing by hand, make sure to capture your thoughts. This is a how-to guide, and you are responsible for doing the work if that's how you choose to use it!

2 **Read each part and reflect** on what personal branding means to you. Start doing the activities.

3 **Get to work**. Each chapter will guide you through self-discovery exercises, but don't worry – it won't deep-dive into childhood traumas (there are plenty of other resources for that). Instead, it will help you examine what's already in your briefcase to prepare for the next steps.

4 **Reference-check your learnings**. Do the activities with a trusted friend, coach or colleague to ensure you're on the right track.

5 **Revisit and reassess**. Life changes, so check back periodically to ensure your personal brand still aligns with who you are and how your life is developing.

You don't necessarily need to follow each chapter chronologically, but if you're new to personal branding, reading the book from beginning to end will strengthen your knowledge and understanding of it. Here's the breakdown:

- **Chapter One**: Understanding what's inside your briefcase – this chapter is about exploring your networking style, personal presence, inspirations and what makes you uniquely you.

- **Chapter Two**: Designing and defining your briefcase – this chapter is about gaining clarity on your driving forces, strengths and areas for mastery.

- **Chapter Three**: Carry your briefcase – here, we will explore your partnerships in life and business to determine how you show up as the best version of you, consistently. It's a marathon, not a sprint.

- **Chapter Four**: Amplify your briefcase – this chapter explores how to create your online presence, aligning your personal brand with the digital world.

Okay, now you know what you can expect from each chapter and what it's all about. Before we start unpacking and building your briefcase, we have one very important question to answer, as it's a core pillar of our journey.

What does 'authenticity' really mean?

Authenticity (according to the *Cambridge Dictionary*) is the quality of being true and real. In a world that values perfection and strong fronts, it can be quite contradictory to be authentic. Unfortunately, society has raised us to be people-pleasers instead of truth-tellers. We've been raised to believe that fitting in with the group is more important than standing out. (Those who know, know.)

This impacts our human need to be part of a tribe, and if that means being aligned with inauthentic people to get their needs met or to obtain 'success', then people will adapt. Why do I say this? It's because I see the impact on businesses and leaders who surround themselves with these kinds of people... there might be some short-term gain. Still, in the long run, there are reasons we are seeing a mental health crisis globally and companies shutting down.

I used to think I had to be liked by everyone, but now I have accepted that inauthentic people cannot thrive around me, nor do I want them to. That's why they say your network is your net worth, and *damn*, it pays off to be surrounded by people who truly have your back in the tough and joyous times (goodbye, tall poppy syndrome[3]). Growing any business will push you to grow yourself, and the type of people you have around you will impact your success (and success, we will explore, is more than financial – yes, some people succeed financially without being authentic – but that's not the kind of success this book is about).

'How you climb a mountain is more important than reaching the top.'

YVON CHOUINARD
founder of Patagonia, Inc.

---

3 'Tall Poppy Syndrome, an Australian cultural expression, describes a "disease" that feeds on the belief that anyone who appears to represent success, high ability or admirable qualities must be attacked, demeaned, and cut down to the common level.' (Mancl & Penington 2011: 79).

Being authentic is not a trait you are born with; anyone can work on it. It's acknowledging your flaws and insecurities, showing up for yourself and others, not taking things so personally, knowing when it is best to speak and when not to, knowing your triggers,[4] taking responsibility for your actions, laughing at yourself, walking away from things that don't align with your values (if able to), asking for help, knowing you are enough and recognising that this is ongoing work, not a one off (acknowledging this is extra hard for people who have been living in survival mode for long periods, who don't feel safe in their own skin).

Being authentic all the time isn't easy. But the more you understand yourself, the more clearly you'll walk, act and think – and bit by bit, that alignment will start to feel more natural.

Before we jump in, let's explore the 'what' and 'why' of personal branding.

What is personal branding, and why does it matter?

Personal branding is an intentional, strategic practice in which you define and express your own value proposition. 'It's the amalgamation of the associations, beliefs, feelings, attitudes, and expectations that people collectively hold about you,' according to Jill Avery and Rachel Greenwald writing in the *Harvard Business Review*.[5] It's based on the outside perception of you.

---

4   A stimulus, like a sound, smell or situation, that can evoke a strong emotional or physical reaction, often associated with a past traumatic experience.

5   Jill Avery and Rachel Greenwald, *Gianpiero Petriglieri. A New Approach to Building Your Personal Brand*. Harvard Business Review, May 2023. Available at: https://hbr.org/2023/05/a-new-approach-to-building-your-personal-brand.

Personal branding is carried with you throughout your life. It's the way that your essence, the best version of you, partners with this commercial world we live in. A personal brand can be interpreted in many different ways; the way I will explain and approach it in this book goes beyond your job title, company, or even who you partnered with. It stays with you no matter what happens in life. It's your demeanour, reputation, work ethic, style, the company you keep and how you operate; it's your social capital, the weight of your word and your ability to influence.

I found that a personal brand was a great avenue for personal development work while also building a career, figuring out how to make money and doing what you care about.

Personal branding can help you build credibility, grow your network, create business opportunities, attract partnerships, achieve your career goals, and more. Now remember that once global access to an audience was only available through selective media channels, but now anyone with a phone or computer can curate, embrace and take advantage of a global audience.

A strong personal brand allows outsiders to get a peek inside your mind, how you think, what you care about, and what your drivers are; it's a way of building rapport with those who are watching, the same way that so many of us build rapport unknowingly or knowingly with superstars and entrepreneurs who are constantly in the public eye. But why do we have paparazzi, and why are they so invasive? We already see enough of these celebrities on television. For the average person, such intrusion would be considered stalking. What drives this obsession to learn about the personal lives of public figures?

For so long, these private aspects of life were shrouded in mystery, existing only in tabloids and scandals. But why do they matter to us? We seek to cultivate a deeper relationship with those we admire – those who receive special treatment or hold prestigious positions. Yet, we often experience disappointment or even schadenfreude.[6] A famous or highly accomplished person is just as susceptible to the human experiences of love, heartbreak, ego, loss and illness, regardless of their wealth, fame, or access to opportunities we may desire. These days, people are more interested in the stories of other people than in following companies pushing a brand agenda.

Individual vs Brand Social Media Followers (2025 Data)

INDIVIDUAL VS BRAND	INSTAGRAM	TWITTER (X)	TIKTOK	LINKEDIN
RICHARD BRANSON	~4.9M	~12M	-	~18M
VIRGIN GROUP	~500K	~1M	~200K	~1M
KIM KARDASHIAN	~357M	~75M	~9.9M	-
SKIMS	~6M	~140K	~1.5M	~216K
CRISTIANO RONALDO	~651M	~115M	~60M	-
CR7 (BRAND)	~10.7M	-	-	-
OPRAH WINFREY	~22.5M	~41M	~327K	~1.3M
OWNTV	~1.4M	~911K	~183K	~64K

It is pretty clear from the above chart that people enjoy connecting and experiencing the stories of people rather than companies. People enjoy getting to know you, especially if their life is vastly different from yours! The difference

---

6   A German word that describes the experience of pleasure, joy or satisfaction that comes from witnessing the troubles, failures, pain, suffering or humiliation of another person.

now is that the internet and social media have provided us with several mediums to access a global audience. There are many positives to this, including the democratisation of knowledge and opportunities, as well as negatives, including mental health decline, comparison culture and abuse.

Also, the days when we were stuck with one company and were known by very few people are disappearing. As technology continues to evolve and the world becomes more connected, showcasing your skills will help you stand out and gain broader opportunities in life and work.

Remember, whatever you post online is a digital tattoo, an imprint on the internet. This means if you are applying for a role or want to become more of a vocal advocate, this could be a factor in whether you are chosen for an opportunity.

I know people who have an incredible online persona, but when I've met them in real life they are so different (and not in a great way). In a time when you can curate whoever you want to be online, with the right tools and enough time, it's tempting to wear the mask. But please, don't take the easy way out. It breaks trust.

Authenticity, even though more difficult, is what creates consistency and consistency is how the market learns to trust you.

'Everyday people don't have the luxury of PR agencies; it is very "Do it Yourself."
When it's genuine, it resonates.'

VINISHA RATHOD

How to DIY a personal brand

Many of my clients struggle to articulate their value, market their skills or business, and develop a genuine presence. The younger generation is embracing their online presence and landing opportunities with their favourite brands by building a following around their personal brand (or, as we are seeing more and more, user-generated content). From my experience, I have found that many of us (especially if you are over thirty) fear putting ourselves out there, especially when it comes to work.

People who are bold and don't ruminate on what others think tend to get more opportunities. It took me years to curate a life where I feel deeply content, not complacent, and balanced across all aspects – all while having fun. I no longer feel the need to escape my life. One of the most rewarding moments is witnessing the light in my client's eyes when they uncover their true essence – who they are, what is blocking them from living to their full potential and how they want to spend their waking hours.

Uncovering your personal brand and finding meaning doesn't have to be this big, hairy, audacious goal; it's a conscious choice. There are countless books on this topic, but today I invite you to join me in exploring what's inside your briefcase and feel the effect when you do. What do you have to lose? The goal is to put you in the driver's seat, empowering you to take ownership of your well-being across different dimensions.

Together, we will walk through actionable steps to bring this to life. For now, give yourself permission to explore.

CHAPTER SUMMARY

- **Personal branding as self-discovery:** This book isn't just about building a brand; it's about uncovering the real you, gaining clarity on what you want, and curating a life you actually enjoy living in all the time, not only when you go on holidays or dabble in escapism.

- **Who this book is for:** Whether you're overwhelmed, feeling lost or navigating a career shift, this book is designed to help you take control of your career and live intentionally, no matter your circumstances.

- **The power of authenticity:** Success isn't about finding a grand purpose; it's about showing up as the best version of yourself, in environments where you can thrive. The book provides a step-by-step guide to help you align your personal and professional life through self-awareness and strategic action.

REFLECTION QUESTIONS

- Do you have a favourite artist or public figure you admire? Why? Do they have a business attached to their name? Do you prefer their personal or business presence?

- What do you hope to achieve once you start actively building your brand?

- What anchors do you have in place so you don't get swept away by success or difficult periods?

CHAPTER 1

UNPACK

People respond well to those
that are sure of what they want.

ANNA WINTOUR
editor-in-chief of American *Vogue*

H AVE YOU EVER met someone completely unaware of how they come across – someone oblivious to their impact on others? Maybe it's a colleague, a boss or even a friend. They move through the world without recognising how their words, actions or energy shape their environment. Now imagine building a business with that person.

Recently, in an interview, I was asked, 'What is the biggest red flag in a founder or business owner?' My answer was, 'An inability to reflect.' A complete lack of self-awareness can be detrimental to a leader and everyone around them. Whether positively or negatively, the way we show up matters and causes us either immense joy or grief.

When starting a business, you're not just committing to a venture; you're stepping into a long-term relationship with co-founders, investors, employees and even customers, so your level of self-awareness impacts your reputation and success. I have sat in a number of co-founder conflicts and heard horrendous stories about business owners' abuse and misalignment, which ultimately ended the company but also impacted relationships and future prospects professionally and financially. This is all character-building to a point, but why learn through suffering? Especially if that part can be a choice.

That's not to say success is impossible without self-awareness – plenty of businesses succeed despite their leaders lacking it. However, in the era of AI, when technology and human connection intertwine like never before, self-awareness is a competitive advantage. The most impactful leaders don't just build companies; they cultivate movements. That often means recognising which parts of yourself you might need to adapt – not erase, but refine – to create something bigger than yourself.

Some of the most iconic figures, such as Steve Jobs (co-founder of Apple), understood the balance between vision and execution. Jobs was known for his uncompromising standards and bold ideas, but he also surrounded himself with talented individuals who could translate that vision into reality.[7] People are often willing to work with tough leaders if they are clear, consistent and transparent. What's far more difficult is working with someone who is deeply insecure, unsure of themselves or – worse – pretending to be someone they're not.

Self-discovery as a secret lever

That's why I urge you to treat self-discovery as your secret weapon. If you're not already in the driver's seat of your own self-awareness, it's time to put on your binoculars and find

---

7   Investopedia. 'The Story of Steve Jobs and Apple.' *Investopedia*, https://www.investopedia.com/articles/fundamental-analysis/12/steve-jobs-apple-story.asp. .

your briefcase. The people who know their strengths are not afraid of others (because it is impossible to be great at everything).

For some, this idea of 'unpacking your briefcase' might be new. For me, self-exploration started early. By the age of six, I was already delving into my psyche. My father was on a mission to uncover the meaning of life, and our family followed suit. As Fijian Indian Hindus, we explored the teachings of Paramahansa Yogananda (my father's guru), Vedic astrology, numerology, colour personalities, love languages, attachment styles – any form of self-development we could find. I was even Reiki One certified by age six (though I had to wait until I was twelve for Reiki Two). This upbringing instilled in me a radical sense of self-responsibility.

How about you? Have you ever stopped to reflect on how your childhood shaped the way you see the world?

Time to unpack

In this chapter, you'll begin unpacking your personal brand – not the polished version that shows up on LinkedIn or résumé, but the deeper version: the way you are in the world. We'll explore your presence, your wellness, your inspirations, and how your mindset shapes your everyday impact. Together, we will:

- Check in with how you are showing up in life right now and how others see you.

- Learn about the inner workings of your mind.

- Explore your style when it comes to personal and networking preferences to better understand how you work best.

This is where the journey begins: with self-awareness, not strategy. Because before you can shape how others see you, you have to see yourself clearly for all your beauty and all your flaws. I'll provide questions and examples to get your thoughts flowing. If you're reading this, chances are you've already started this journey in some way. Let's build on that and connect the dots – you might surprise yourself, in a good way.

EXERCISE
SELF-DISCOVERY

Ask yourself the following questions. You can use this as a journal prompt or simply reflect on each question.

- Why do you want to do this activity?

- Is there anything you want to change about yourself?

- How do you think you are currently perceived? Does it differ between family, friends, colleagues or your partner?

- What do you want your eulogy to say? Does it vary depending on whether your family, friends and/or colleagues read it? What elements do you want to be remembered for?

- What is the biggest compliment someone could give you?

- What is the most insulting thing someone could say to you?

- Who do you admire in your personal and professional circle? And why is this so? List at least three traits as specifically as possible.

How was that experience for you? Was there anything you were surprised by? The eulogy question tends to have similar answers – people want to be remembered as caring and thoughtful, having left a legacy for their loved ones.

A really telling one is the biggest compliment and insult question – it is a great question if you are looking for a conversation starter in any personal or professional setting. For example:

- One of the biggest compliments for me is, 'Vinisha, your food tastes like my grandma's cooking.' Because I show my love through cooking, this is a huge compliment.

- Another one is, 'Vinisha, I can be myself around you,' because I know what it felt like to have to hide and hinder for so long.

Now, on the flip side, if I look at the insults or what really gets to me, here are some things that tend to bug me:

- Being completely ignored or overlooked due to the way I look – this has happened a few times at work. I have become much better at adapting to this; however, it still gets to me.

- Being noticed for all the wrong reasons; as an object to be gazed at rather than someone who has something to contribute. Again, times are changing; however, this still gets to me.

By understanding what is important to me, I make an effort in my own work to counter these experiences and curate environments and spaces where people can be noticed and respected for the right reasons. I know many people from similar backgrounds feel the same way.

Keep track of how you answered those questions, as it will be very useful when you do the next exercises in this chapter. Imagine these questions as the guide, filled with clues on how you want your personal brand to show up and what you care about. Keep an eye out for red herrings!

Alignment check

I have met many people who have access to wealth and are incredibly fit, yet they lack mental, social and spiritual fulfillment. Too often, I see them drawn into unhealthy relationships or even harmful groups (cults), becoming a lesser version of themselves in their desperate search for belonging or an escape from their thoughts.

I share this with you to pose a question: What if you could create a life you don't need to escape from? How do you build a life where you feel alive every single day? Not only when you achieve a certain goal, but also if you already have? This part is about checking in on where you are in life right now to identify some areas that might need more focused love and attention.

This will not be the bulk of the book, as it's mainly focused on your career, but as you build your career, you want to be aware of how other parts of your life are falling into place. Think of this as similar to a performance review, but led by you. It's a moment to reflect on what's going well, what's feeling off and what needs attention. A gentle reminder – this book is not a substitute for medical or psychological advice. If anything here brings something up for you, please do reach out to a qualified health professional. You deserve proper support.

EXERCISE
ALIGNMENT CHECK

Here are some questions to help you understand how you feel across these different dimensions. How would you rate each area out of ten? This also helps identify what you may need to focus on to support you with your personal brand and living a more fulfilled life.

DIMENSION	QUESTIONS	RATING 1–10
Physically	• How would you rate your overall health? • How often do you exercise? Can you walk up a flight of stairs without losing your breath? • What ailments or physical challenges do you currently face? Are they due to other factors such as illness, menopause, andropause? • What changes, if any, do you need to make to improve your physical well-being?	
Financially	• What is your relationship with money? • Is there anything you want to improve about your financial situation? • Do you have enough to cover your basic survival needs? • Do you have a source of passive income? • Do others depend on you financially? • Could you afford an unexpected major expense?	
Mentally	• How would you describe your state of mind? • How do you handle setbacks and challenges? • How do you deal with pain, uncertainty and change? • Do you have a place you can recharge?	
Socially	• How satisfied are you with your social circles, friendships and partnerships? • Are the people in your life reliable and supportive? • Do they encourage your growth and bring out the best in you, or do they have the opposite effect? • Do you connect with your circle enough? Is there anything you want to change?	
Spiritually	• What gets you out of bed? • What do you deeply care about? • Is there anything/anyone who helps you during the tough times?	

Identifying the stories attached to each of these dimensions can help reveal areas to work on, as each area plays a vital role in a life filled with vitality, joy and autonomy. Our relationship with our body – our essence's home – is especially important to nurture. Remember, the sole reason for the body is to keep you alive, and it will send signals to you when its needs aren't being met.

The importance of managing your brain

Managing your brain isn't just about being productive or performing well – it's essential for your mental health and resilience in the face of life's challenges. Let's face it, it's not always happy times; life is filled with ups and downs. This concept of continuous learning – of knowing yourself and finding what brings you back amidst chaos – is crucial in navigating personal ups and downs (especially if you want to live in this commercial world!). Similar to the muscle of critical thinking, it becomes harder to face challenges with a clear mind if you don't exercise it.

When we feel overwhelmed or under threat, the *amygdala* – the brain's emotional alarm system – activates our fight, flight, freeze or fawn response. In that moment, the logical part of the brain (the *prefrontal cortex*) is effectively bypassed, making it harder to think clearly or respond rationally. This is known as an *amygdala hijack*, a term popularised by Daniel Goleman in *Emotional Intelligence.*[8]

I wouldn't share this if I didn't apply it to myself when experiencing tough moments, such as my father's passing, heartbreaks, divorce, and the trials and tribulations of setting up my own business.

Why is this important? Managing how you respond to situations will help you become the driver and decision-maker

---

8   Goleman, D. (1995). *Emotional Intelligence: Why It Can Matter More Than IQ.* Bantam Books.

of your own life. If you're not grounded in yourself and taking care of your essence (that's you as you exist in this world), then growing your personal brand will be more challenging. How are you taking care of yourself, and what habits would you like to change to live a healthier life?

Sometimes, calming the brain isn't just about *thinking differently* – it's also about *feeling differently*. That's where your brain chemistry steps in.

The four happy hormones

In between sensing and responding to a situation, chemicals called neurotransmitters and hormones help your brain understand, evaluate and communicate what you're experiencing. These various neurotransmitters and hormones have specific jobs – each being activated in a certain way, signalling certain emotions and stimulating certain areas of your brain.

Think of these hormones (dopamine, serotonin, endorphins and oxytocin) as your internal support team. Knowing how to activate them can help improve your mood and emotional state, and foster a more positive mindset, greater emotional resilience and a greater sense of well-being.[9] Here's a brief breakdown, along with suggestions for how to boost each one or all.

---

9   McCallum, K. (2021, September 13). *Brain Chemistry & Your Mood: 4 Hormones That Promote Happiness*. Houston Methodist On Health. Retrieved from https://www.houston methodist.org/blog/articles/2021/sep/brain-chemistry-your-mood-4-hormones-that-promote-happiness.

Watson, S. (2024, April 18). *Feel-good hormones: How they affect your mind, mood, and body*. Harvard Health Publishing. Retrieved from https://www.health.harvard.edu/mind-and-mood/feel-good-hormones-how-they-affect-your-mind-mood-and-body.

CBHS Health Fund. (2021, August 15). *Understanding the chemicals controlling your mood*. Retrieved from https://www.cbhs.com.au/mind-and-body/blog/understanding-the-chemicals-controlling-your-mood.

Dopamine (The 'feel good' hormone)

- **Role**: Dopamine is involved in motivation, pleasure and reward. It's the reason why certain activities (eating your favourite foods or scrolling social media) feel so satisfying. It is responsible for memory, mood, sleep, learning, concentration, libido and movement, so it is important to have the right amount of it, as it plays a big role in controlling your impulses and addictions.[10]

- **Boost**: Set small, achievable goals, and celebrate your wins (even the small ones) and reward yourself for completing tasks. Try something new that excites you, get proper sleep, exercise, eat a healthy diet, listen to music and meditate.

- **Prompt**: What activities tend to give me a quick dopamine hit? Do they serve me in the long run, or do they distract me from my bigger goals?

Serotonin (The 'mood regulator' hormone)

- **Role**: Serotonin is one of the natural body chemicals that controls your mood, memory and stress responses, as well as how you feel pain, addiction and sexual desire.[11] When you have adequate levels of serotonin, you feel emotionally stable and calm, and you'll also have noticeably higher levels of energy and focus. When you have too little serotonin, it can impact sleep, the digestive system, phobias, depression, anxiety and even suicide.

- **Boost**: Spend time outdoors, practise kindness to yourself and others, engage in regular physical activity, therapy

---

10 Healthdirect Australia. (n.d.). *Dopamine*. Retrieved from https://www.healthdirect.gov. au/dopamine.

11 Healthdirect Australia. (n.d.). *Serotonin*. Retrieved from https://www.healthdirect.gov. au/serotonin.

and meditation, and eat foods that support serotonin production (those rich in tryptophan).

- **Prompt**: When do I feel happiest? What environments or activities tend to boost my serotonin levels?

Endorphins (The 'natural painkiller' hormone)

- **Role**: Endorphins reduce pain and boost feelings of happiness and confidence. They help you cope with stress and discomfort by releasing the chemical during an act. About twenty different types of endorphins exist, which are released when we laugh, fall in love, have sex, and even eat a delicious meal.

- **Boost**: Exercise, laughter, acupuncture, sunlight or anything that gets your body moving (dancing or hiking). Indulge in dark chocolate and wine, watch dramas or take a hot bath.[12]

- **Prompt**: What activities make me feel energised and joyful, even after a challenging day? What activities, situations and people help me become more confident?

Oxytocin (The 'love and connection' hormone)

- **Role**: Oxytocin is a natural hormone made and stored in the brain, and is released when you bond with others, creating a sense of trust and deep connection (e.g., eye contact).[13] Oxytocin is essential for relationships and emotional intimacy as it plays a key role in building

---

12 Cafasso, J. (2020, December 2). *How to Boost Your Morning Endorphin Levels: 7 Ways.* Healthline. Retrieved from https://www.healthline.com/health/mental-health/boost-your-morning-endorphin-level.

13 Healthdirect Australia. (n.d.). *Oxytocin.* Retrieved from https://www.healthdirect.gov.au/oxytocin.

connections, parent-infant bonding, romance and recognising one another.

- **Boost**: Spend time with loved ones, engage in physical
  touch (hugging, massage), listen to music or spend time
  with animals.

- **Prompt**: Who makes me feel loved and connected? How
  can I nurture these relationships to feel supported? How
  do I feel when someone looks directly into my eyes versus when I can't see their eyes?

Looking after your hormone squad

I explain the feeling of being grounded as a way to connect
with your hormone squad (who are wired to keep you alive).
When you feel overwhelmed, finding something that brings you
back and out of your overthinking/anxious head is essential.

When I worked as an executive assistant to CEOs and
Boards, I would ask this question and if they didn't know
how to reset I would send them out for walks or set aside
time for their lunch to help clear their mind. Heard of happy
wife, happy life? The same goes for a boss – happy CEO,
happy workplace.

When I was going through a particularly difficult period
in my life, I actively engaged in HIIT (high intensity inter-
val training), therapy, acupuncture and human behaviour
coaching sessions (thanks team). I also actively changed my
diet, environment and social circle. I know from lived experience that looking after your hormone squad will help you
get through life's toughest moments.

Coping mechanisms

Each of us has ways we like to reset. Here are some examples of how healthy coping mechanisms help me reset:

- **The rocking chair**: I grew up with a rocking chair, and to this day I find solace in that gentle swaying movement – whether it's being on a boat or sitting on my mother's home *julwa* (seat swing).

- **Music**: Music is another pillar of my well-being – whether it's Hare Krishna mantras, Deep House, or Hans Zimmer's soundtrack for the film *Gladiator*. We remember sound from the womb; we hear before we see, taste or smell.

- **Laughter**: Social media algorithms serve up humour that resonates with me, but I stay mindful of the fine line between healthy entertainment and doom-scrolling. I also have the funniest friends, so laughter is the best way to get me out of my head.

- **Exercise and nature**: I try to go to my local gym four to five times a week or go swimming in the ocean. Luckily, I live a bus ride from Bondi Beach, so I try to go there or hike or walk to connect with nature.

- **Dopamine Fridays**: I allocate a half or full day on Friday, depending on what I have on, to go do something I enjoy that usually involves hugging a baby or puppy, going to the beach, grabbing lunch with a friend or kayaking.

- **Prayer**: When I go through the darkest times, I often find myself praying. As an 'allofist' (someone who prays to all gods), sometimes I pray in a church, temple, by the water or at home.[14]

- **Learning something new**: If I am feeling stifled or over-whelmed, I will put on a podcast or read a book, especially if I need to understand why someone operates in a particular way.

---

14 Acknowledging Omnism (which is a belief in all religions) which I only learnt about very recently. I personally say 'allofism', so I will stick with that word.

- **Buying flowers**: I have a non-negotiable ritual (even when I was married) to buy flowers from the markets every week – they remind me of nature's beauty and life's impermanence.

- **Calling/reaching out**: Remember, we are communal, so it's okay to lean on each other. There is a positive effect to hugging and hearing a soothing voice – sometimes it's my mum, other times I call my nieces, or sometimes I want a belly laugh with my friends. Popularised by Simon Sinek, an eight-minute conversation is more than enough to make a person feel heard, to reassure us that someone is there for us.

- **Cooking**: I love the taste of my own cooking and experiencing the results of my creation.

- **Travel**: When I am stifled, I enjoy stretching my brain by going somewhere new and absorbing myself in another world.

- **Poetry**: When I am overwhelmed or deeply sad, and my essence wants to speak, I am drawn to writing poetry. I wrote a lot when I was very young, and I am getting back into it.

Mapping your stimuli and identifying what grounds you

Now it's your turn! In your daily life, you are constantly surrounded by stimuli that trigger different emotional and physical reactions. It's important to map out how you're spending your time, what habits are serving you, and which ones may be taking you away from your true self.

One of the first steps in taking the driver's seat of your life is becoming aware of how you spend your time and your forms of escapism and coping. Dr Marny Lishman shared that 'Excessive dopamine releases can lead to addictions, where the person automatically keeps doing the behaviour – despite the physical or psychological consequences.'[15]

That's why, once we try one of those cookies, we might come back for another one (or two or three). The darker side of dopamine is the intense feeling of reward people feel when they engage in activities such as recreational drug use, gambling, doom-scrolling social media, gaming excessively or abusing alcohol. If you have an addiction that needs to be treated, please see a specialist. This activity aims to identify how you are spending your time so you can decide how you want to manage it to meet your goals.

'We may not be responsible for the way the world creates our mind, but we can learn to take responsibility for the mind with which we create our world.'

DR GABOR MATÉ

15   Lishman, M. (2023, May 24). *Could a dopamine detox make you happier?* Australian Psychological Society. Retrieved from https://psychology.org.au/about-us/news-and-media/aps-in-the-media/2023/could-a-dopamine-detox-make-you-happier.

ACTIVITY
CREATE YOUR OWN
STIMULATION MAP

Step 1: Consider all the activities you engage in throughout your day. This could include anything from how you wake up to how you unwind at night. Here's a suggested approach to go about it:

Make a list of things that stimulate you during any day (no need to judge yourself; this is an awareness exercise). Stimuli in your day could be anything from social media scrolling to emotional eating. Please feel free to chop and change and tailor this exercise to you.

1. MORNING ROUTINE:

- Do you check your phone? If so, which apps?
- Do you start your day with social media, emails and news?
- Do you engage in a morning ritual (meditation, exercise, journaling)?
- Do you consume caffeine or other stimulants?

2. ON YOUR COMMUTE:

- Do you listen to podcasts, music or news during your commute?
- Do you scroll through social media during travel?
- Do you connect with a person regularly on your commute? Or speak with strangers?
- Do you feel anxious, rushed or frustrated during your commute?
- Do you engage in deep thinking or personal reflection while commuting?

3. DURING WORK HOURS:

- How do you use your breaks? Do you scroll through social media or check emails?
- Do you check your phone frequently?
- Do you snack while working? If so, what types of food?
- Do you listen to music or podcasts during work?
- How do you manage distractions or procrastination?
- How do you feel about your colleagues?
- Do you prefer working under pressure? Or having a plan?

4. WHILE COOKING OR PREPARING FOOD:

- Do you snack while preparing meals?
- Do you listen to music, podcasts or news while cooking?
- Do you find cooking therapeutic or a chore?
- Are there any specific food choices that provide emotional comfort while cooking?

5. EVENING ROUTINE:

- Do you unwind with TV, games, podcasts or binge-watching a series?
- Do you check social media or email in the evenings?
- Do you eat dinner while watching TV or on your phone?
- Do you engage in any calming activities (e.g., reading, baths, meditation)?

6. BEFORE YOU GO TO SLEEP:

- Do you play games or scroll social media?
- Do you engage in relaxing activities such as reading, listening to calming music or watching TV?
- Do you check emails or respond to work-related messages?
- Do you drink something stimulating (e.g., coffee, energy drinks)?

7. SOCIAL SITUATIONS:

- How do you spend time with friends or family?
- Do you enjoy shopping, eating out or watching movies together?
- Do you find certain conversations or behaviours (e.g., gossip, excessive drinking) cause an emotional trigger?
- Do you use social media to stay connected with friends, or is it more about observing?
- Do you have particular friends or people who bring out the best in you? What is it about some people who bring out the best versus worst version of you?

8. WHEN IN A STATE OF OVERWHELM:

- Do you reach for emotional comfort food?
- Do you distract yourself with social media, gaming or TV?
- Do you go into 'avoidance mode' by scrolling or gaming?
- Do you tend to isolate yourself or reach out for support?
- How do you bring yourself out of a spiral?

9. OUT AND ABOUT (NETWORKING, PERSONAL, HOBBIES OR SOCIAL EVENTS):

- Are you constantly checking your phone during social events or meetings?
- Do you engage in networking to build connections?
- Do you seek approval or validation from others during social gatherings?
- Do you drink alcohol or consume stimulants at these events?
- Do you regularly engage in a hobby that you enjoy (e.g., sports, music)?

10. TIME ALONE/WEEKENDS:

- How do you spend your time alone (e.g., reading, binge-watching, scrolling, working out)?
- Do you feel pressure to always be productive when by yourself?
- Do you follow a self-care routine when you have time to yourself?
- Do you seek quiet time for reflection, meditation or mindfulness?

11. AROUND FAMILY OR LOVED ONES:

- Do you feel comfortable being yourself or do you act differently around family?
- How do you connect with your family – through conversation, activities or food?
- Are there certain family dynamics that create emotional responses (e.g., stress, frustration, joy)?
- Do you feel more relaxed or stressed when with family?

12. WHILE TRAVELLING:

- Do you use travel as an escape from everyday life?
- Do you have a favourite holiday memory? Why was it so special?
- What activities do you enjoy doing on holidays (e.g., eating, shopping, sightseeing)?
- Do you tend to relax on holidays or fill up the calendar with multiple activities?
- When you return home, do you need a holiday after your holiday?

Step 2: Rate each activity as helpful or harmful

Once you identify the stimuli that occupy your time, put the approximate time spent next to them in your notes. This will help you to identify if it is helpful or harmful, and see if there is anything you want to change.

- **Helpful**: This activity contributes positively to your emotional well-being, boosts your mood, helps you relax or aligns with your personal goals. It may help you recharge, feel more productive or stay grounded.

- **Harmful**: This activity drains you, contributes to stress, distracts you from important tasks, or leaves you feeling unfulfilled or negative. It could be a behaviour that feels like an escape but doesn't serve your well-being in the long run.

HERE IS AN EXAMPLE:

- Check phone for news/social media – Harmful (distraction, mind starts racing)

- Go to the gym/exercise – Helpful (movement is hormone squad medicine)

- Go to the beach – Helpful (nature, ocean is helpful)

- Excessive alcohol – Harmful (temporary coping measure, can't handle hangovers)

Again: please do not judge yourself. This is all about awareness. The coping mechanisms were created once upon a time to help you cope, but you are in the driver's seat to change them if they're harming you.

REFLECTION AND NEXT STEPS

- After rating your activities, ask yourself: Are there any activities I should reduce or remove from my day to make space for more helpful ones?

- Do any activities that I marked as harmful have a specific trigger, stress or anxiety? What can I replace those with to feel that I might enjoy being alive?

- How do I feel after engaging in the 'helpful' activities versus the 'harmful' ones? What patterns do I notice?

- Are there particular environments and/or people that bring out the best in me versus the worst? Why is this so?

- When you were younger and overwhelmed, was there an activity that helped you feel calm? (You can bring back things such as playing, colouring, drawing, etc.)

This exercise will help you gain awareness of how your daily activities impact your emotional and physical well-being and empower you to make more intentional choices moving forward. I often tell clients to put the activities that help them on their phone or their fridge as a mental prompt to remind them how they want to spend their time, especially when they feel overwhelmed.

Understanding the stimuli in our lives allows us to recognise patterns and make informed choices about spending our time and energy. By identifying which activities bring us back to a grounded state and distinguishing between helpful and harmful stimuli, we can better support our mental health and well-being, which in turn impacts our decision-making.

Whether through physical exercise, spending time with loved ones, finding joy in small accomplishments, or simply laughing, there are many ways to nurture your essence from within. Similar to building muscle or forming a habit, managing your brain and your emotions is something that can be trained and refined over time. This self-awareness enables us to create a more balanced and fulfilling life that aligns with our values, goals and priorities.

A moment to learn about your community

From birth, we are part of groups – families, communities, schools, workplaces and social circles. These groups shape our understanding of the world, offering identity and security. We unconsciously adopt their values, beliefs and behaviours to remain included. Most of the time, this happens seamlessly because we're surrounded by people who think and act similarly. Whether it's a family tradition, an unspoken workplace culture or a long-standing social expectation, we stay connected by following the rules.

But what happens when someone challenges these norms? When they start questioning traditions, making different choices or stepping outside the group's expectations?

Often the response isn't open dialogue, but shame. This can be as subtle as quiet disapproval, overt ridicule or exclusion. The emotional weight can be overwhelming, making it easier for most people to conform rather than risk rejection. But what if someone refuses to fall back in line? Have you ever felt the tension of going against the group in a work or family setting? How did you navigate it?

Neuropsychologist Dr Mario Martinez, author of *The Mind-Body Code*, has studied the impact of social rejection and found that tribal shaming can lead to serious mental and physical consequences, from chronic stress to illness.

What's surprising is that this pressure doesn't always come from cruelty – it often stems from a protective instinct. Groups thrive on stability, and when one person changes, it disrupts the system. To maintain order, the community applies social pressure to pull them back in.

Shame, in this way, becomes a tool for keeping people in line, as there is safety in what is known.

The tragedy is that this fear of rejection can prevent people from becoming the best version of themselves. Many sacrifice their hopes and dreams to remain accepted, and while the community may welcome them back this often comes at a price. The unfortunate reality is that most groups prefer predictability over evolution, making it difficult for individuals to break free.[16] Who is a part of your social circle, and how do they influence you?

How do others see you?

Now that we have touched on your community, let us hear from them! Please note, feedback from your circle is a tool for insight, not external validation – final decisions rest on authentic alignment with your own values. Reach out to people you have worked with or opinions you deeply trust, using the four questions and template below, or you can simply do a personality test online, such as Myers-Briggs, Human Design,   alities, Enneagram, or many others.

---

16 Martinez, M. (2014). *The MindBody Code: How to Change the Beliefs That Limit Your Health, Longevity, and Success.* Sounds True.

EXERCISE
HOW AM I PERCEIVED?

I recommend asking four or five people to answer the following questions about you. You can do this by email, text or over the phone, and you can do it yourself or through another person. Make sure you record the results.

- What are my greatest strengths?
- Why do you like spending time with me?
- If you could share one piece of advice to help me reach my full thriving potential, what would that be?
- If money, location or connections were no object, what kind of environment and job do you see me doing my best work in?

How did you find that activity, and was there anything that surprised you? This is an excellent activity to help you recognise your superpowers. This will also help you decide if the personality tests you've done have been accurate. You want the people you ask to engage in this process with you to be as honest as possible – you might be surprised why people like spending time with you!

How do you show up at work?

A powerful exercise in uncovering and designing your briefcase is identifying the aspects of your past jobs that you genuinely enjoyed. By reviewing your last few roles, you'll likely find a common thread – this is especially helpful for generalists or those of you who have had multiple careers. Recognising these patterns provides clarity on what to focus on next. Equally important is identifying what you didn't enjoy, as this helps you pinpoint elements to seek out or avoid in future roles.

This exercise also equips you with the right questions to ask when considering a new employer, co-founder or investment opportunity. Certain aspects of a business are fundamental and will inevitably shape your experience in the workplace. Understanding these factors allows you to make more-informed decisions and align yourself with environments that bring out your best.

As someone who specialises in people, culture and growth, I've seen firsthand how much your environment influences how you show up. Rather than letting external factors dictate your experience, take stock of your past roles and reflect on what truly worked – and what didn't – so you can make deliberate decisions and move forward intentionally.

EXERCISE
REFLECTING ON
YOUR WORK HISTORY

Reflect on the following questions to help you determine which environments you work in best.

- What did I enjoy about the last four or five roles?
- Were there particular parts of a role for which I received consistently good feedback?
- Were there parts of my job that I found easy to do compared to others?

- Was there something I didn't enjoy and why?
- Were there any behaviours that I was surprised by (positively or negatively)?
- Which mentor(s) (at work or in your circle) had the biggest impact on me, and what made their support or guidance meaningful?

How to draw up your findings (specifics are great – they highlight what is important).

ENJOYED – EXAMPLES:
- Interesting problems to solve
- Great culture and leaders
- Role had a lot of autonomy and agency
- Office location
- Learning opportunities
- Financial stability
- Flexibility – e.g., able to pursue training for the Olympics

DISLIKED – EXAMPLES:
- Hands-off founder/business leader (no clear direction)
- Bureaucracy and excessive administration (new ideas were not welcomed)
- Awful manager – micromanagement and lots of hierarchy
- Remote only and distant from the team
- Lack of control over outcomes and end products

To help with the next part, gather those experiences and identify common threads or themes. As we define your superpowers, these insights will be valuable in the next chapter. You may have noticed some recurring patterns, including a strong sense of community, great managers who know how to bring out the best in their teams or environments that felt frustrating, such as those requiring excessive stakeholder management or slow decision-making.

You'll be surprised by what you may find when you dive into the environments and the leaders that influenced them. Often, the qualities you admire in others reflect traits you possess or aspire to develop. I deeply admired a mentor who balanced kindness with the ability to set firm boundaries – something I've struggled with due to my deep-seated people-pleasing tendencies. Observing her approach highlighted what I value and where I want to grow. Another mentor excelled at delivering constructive feedback and influencing others to embrace change, a skill I recognised as important in the work I want to do.

By identifying these themes, you clarify what truly matters to you and what to nurture and focus on as you move forward.

Your networking style

Let's say it together: people buy people. Why do you think, after all these years, that sales is still an art built on human interaction? Learning how to influence people is a skill that you can develop to help promote and enforce your personal brand, aka your networking style.

So, let's start with defining networking. What do you think of this definition? Networking is building relationships with aligned human beings for mutually beneficial collaboration (thanks Dickie from Hype Man Media).

Now, I want to caveat that not everyone has natural networking skills, but there are definitely ways to learn how you operate in these settings. Remember, your personal brand is carried with you consistently even as you move through jobs and companies, so knowing how you like to show up during this time is an important life skill.

'There is so much power in proximity, but you need to know how to use it.'

VINISHA RATHOD

I know sales and networking are not in everyone's skill set, so we have questions to determine your personal networking style. We network and build relationships all the time, on any social occasion. So, what do you do naturally with family, at friends' gatherings or in wedding settings?

Before I was aware of how I operated, I received criticism both personally and professionally for not working the room, not being widely known, not talking to the right people straight away, not closing deals in the first conversation, or gaining intel on a specific company or deal.

The more I tried to be what others wanted me to be, the more draining it was, and more often than not I left the functions with nothing. I completely denied my natural gift of developing trusted deep relationships, to fit into how other expected me to work.

Have a think about how you currently network and build relationships. There are some questions below to help you start mapping out your natural style and what you may want to continue to do. Depending on what stage of life you are in, you can think of work conferences or personal settings such as weddings and family functions.

EXERCISE
EXPLORE YOUR
NETWORKING STYLE

- When you are about to go to a conference or large gathering, how important is it for you to know beforehand who is going?

- What kind of activities do you do in the lead-up?

- When you enter a room filled with people you don't know, what is the first thing you do?

- What kind of people do you find approachable? Tell me about their character traits. Is there something you notice?

- How about people who are unapproachable or people you want to run away from?

- How easily can you leave a conversation? Do you have a way you can exit? What is your favourite way versus definitely not?

- What is the natural follow-up process after you meet someone?

Your personal style

When it comes to personal brand, for me, personal style makes a big impact. What works in my favour, especially when I am in a new space, is that my personal style is very noticeable, and makes a big difference when I enter social environments. My style makes me immediately interesting, and the people who are too conventional tend to steer clear (we don't typically work well together anyway). Those who are curious make for a very interesting discussion.

I have always had a very distinctive style; a big part of my expression and how I embrace my love for different cultures is through my wardrobe. I have abayas from Saudi Arabia, kimonos from Japan, capes from London, scarves from Italy, boots from Texas and many beautiful Indian outfits that I integrate into my style.

Please know I am not talking about wearing fancy brands and I am a big fan of circular fashion. Anyone who knows me would tell you I don't come from that world. I have fun integrating styles, colours, fun shoes (one set has wings) and quirky earrings. Have you heard of the trend of dopamine dressing? It refers to the practice of dressing in a way that brings you joy and boosts your mood and is something I utilise in my day-to-day life.

Let's explore the role of fashion and how it shows up when you work. It is also important, as we explore, that you need to find what environments you thrive in compared to the professional expectations, depending on the setting. I adjust my fashion style to some environments; for example, I do not wear my 'dead inside' earrings or bring my sticker-covered briefcase when I am working in the Middle East. However, I do add dashes of colour to my abaya. It's all about applying your personal brand strategically for the environments you are in.

Let's figure out how you currently show up at work and in social settings, how you associate yourself with your physical style, and see if this is something you can work on.

EXERCISE
EXPLORE YOUR
PERSONAL STYLE

- Do you have one or two go-to outfits for high-stakes situations such as pitches, interviews, conferences or presentations? What are they, and why do they work for you?

- Which items in your wardrobe do you find yourself reaching for repeatedly during a typical work week? What does that tell you about your current style?

- Are there any clothes, accessories or shoes that instantly shift your mood or mindset when you put them on? What effect do they have (e.g., my winged shoes or glitter coat)?

- Is there anyone in particular whom you admire in terms of how they show up to functions (professional or personal)?

We all associate colours with an emotion or feeling. For example, if I need to have an important meeting, I wear a red jacket, as it helps me become more confident. If I am presenting, then I wear a bright, bold fuchsia (bright purple) outfit, a glittery dress or sparkly shoes. What you wear has an impact on how you look. It's that classic saying that if you look good, then you'll feel good.

How to improve your networking skills

It can be a bit daunting to meet new people. Great research has been done by a popular *TED Talk* speaker, Vanessa van Edwards,[17] who is an expert on body language and communication. She has some tips worth considering as you level up your networking questions. When it comes to sparking conversations, consider changing your approach. You can do this by rephrasing your typical introduction questions.

Instead of asking the typical questions, try the ones on the right:

- What do you do? >> Is there something you are looking forward to or excited by?

- Where are you from? >> Have you learned anything interesting lately?

- How are you? >> What is your biggest goal right now?

Personally, when I network, I share a story about something random and funny that has happened, and we usually talk about something completely different. It's a refreshing way to connect with someone's essence. The briefcase has been a great game-changer, as the typical first question is , 'V, what is in the briefcase?'

Dr John Medina found that when dopamine is triggered by a verbal conversation, it makes a mental note, which makes you more memorable. Basically, when you ask good questions, you're associated with good things.[18]

---

17   Van Edwards, V. (2023, March 15). *Our theme this month is Networking! So here are my favorite 3 questions to elevating new friends to lasting friends and deepening existing friendships and relationships.* LinkedIn. Retrieved from https://www.linkedin.com/posts/vanessavanedwards_our-theme-this-month-is-networking-so-here-activity-7305220428422074368-bK9P.

18   Medina, J. (2008). *Brain Rules: 12 Principles for Surviving and Thriving at Work, Home, and School.* Pear Press.

You don't need a title, a big following or a master plan to have a personal brand. You already have one – it lives in how you speak, how you show up and how you care. By unpacking your presence, your energy, and the way you move through the world, you've taken the first step in reclaiming your story. And that story matters.

In the next chapter, you'll begin to sort through what you've unpacked – clarifying your values, strengths, and what you want your brand to stand for. You've opened the briefcase. Now let's start arranging what belongs in it.

CHAPTER SUMMARY

- **Self-awareness is your secret weapon:** The way you show up – your energy, words and actions – affects how others perceive and engage with you. Especially as we enter the Fourth Industrial Revolution, building self-awareness helps you make intentional choices that align with your personal and professional goals.

- **Your briefcase holds the key to your brand:** Unpacking your personal brand starts with understanding your current state of wellness, mindset, networking style and how others see you. This awareness allows you to define how you want to present yourself and live.

- **Confidence comes from alignment:** The most impactful personal brands aren't created; they're uncovered. By embracing who you truly are and leaning into your strengths and the way you enjoy showing up, you can navigate your career and relationships with clarity, confidence and ease.

REFLECTION QUESTIONS

- Do you have any habits you want to change?

- Reflect on your mentors and past workplaces. What did you enjoy, and what patterns did you notice?

- Review your beliefs about networking/building relationships. How do you like to currently make connections? Do you have a go-to question or fact you like to share?

CHAPTER 2

DESIGN

The most powerful weapon on
Earth is the human soul on fire.

FERDINAND FOCH
French Army general

OST OF US spend years picking up labels, job titles, habits and expectations. But how often do we pause and ask: Am I actually where I want to be? I usually see this happen when something in life stops us in our tracks - separation, a loved one's death, job loss, health, retirement, and so on.

In Chapter 1, you began unpacking your briefcase - getting clear on your presence, wellness, and the energy you bring into a room. Now it's time to make some decisions. What stays? What goes? And what gets placed right at the top, ready to be used?

In this chapter we'll explore timeless skills, how to articulate and commercialise your natural gifts, your values, and your unique way of thinking and contributing. You'll learn how to align your strengths with what drives you - and how to design a personal brand that reflects the real you, not a curated version. We'll unlock your briefcase and start filling it with the strengths and tools you already carry with you. Together we will:

- Dive into the pursuit of mastery framework to determine your mastery and uncover your superpowers and passion.

- Challenge self-doubt to help you walk confidently with your briefcase.

- Identify your core values, your personal needs, and your perfect environment for growth and success.

'Success doesn't come from what you do occasionally. It comes from what you do consistently.'

MARIE FORLEO
entrepreneur, writer and philanthropist

Your pursuit to mastery

Three years ago, when I started working for an executive search firm specialising in finding senior leaders positions in fast-growth tech companies, I noticed that people in the creative and tech community really focused on finding their passion as their main driver for decision-making. This was never something in the corporate world that was really talked about. We carried on and passion wasn't part of the job description, nor was it something that many people were seeking or were able to seek (did people actually love their jobs?).

Making important career or life decisions purely based on passion is naïve, but making decisions and living without any passion or drive leaves many people feeling empty. It's no surprise that I have found myself in several career conversations revolving around 'finding your passion'. But, rather than asking, 'How do you pursue your passion?' the conversation started to evolve to, 'What mastery do you want to pursue?'

The pursuit of mastery framework below can be used to pitch your business, navigate interviews, and connect with potential companies or future employees. In fact, I'd say it's one of the most important parts of this book. It helps you get clear on your *why*, so you can spend your time intentionally and cut through the noise. I use it in almost every conversation when meeting someone new. It instantly sets the tone, shows people where I stand, and either opens the door or doesn't – and that clarity makes life a whole lot simpler.

This kind of clarity is what we will uncover right now, and the great part is that when you are clear, you are not attached to job titles or scared of technological advancements! Together, we'll unpack what mastery means to you and help you define your *drivers* with confidence and conviction.

Mastery

Your mastery: simple to explain, timeless, and industry and role-agnostic. Mastery is a conscious effort to become skilled in something, and a professional muscle you can train and flex over time that usually leads to higher rewards. For example, my mastery is building great places to work.

I do that by pulling organisations apart so I can understand how to help keep them aligned, sustainable and profitable, and ensure an environment where people can thrive. Here are some other examples of mastery that my clients have shared with me:

- Shifting workplace mindsets from 'I' to 'We' – fostering collaboration

- The bridge between technology capabilities, customer and business needs

- Turning around disregarded programs or products

- Using financial and business strategies to scale and transition businesses

- Realigning people and companies to their creative source through education

- Creating practical and inclusive customer experiences

Let's remove the guilt of passion from your career. Consider navigating your career not by job titles, but by the professional muscle you want to grow. So, how does your mastery align with your passion/driver? When you start articulating across the three, this is where you can connect and build your brand both online and offline.

Your passion/driver

What do you care so deeply about that it either provides you with an overwhelming sense of clarity or joy, or makes your blood boil with rage? Now, not everyone has intense drivers relating to social justice. Your driver can be more uplifting or expressed in a very different way.

There are a few key passion areas that people tend to align with, such as animal rights, climate change, equity, social justice, children's rights, financial literacy, health, and more. Here are some client examples:

- Express life's beauty through creativity, art, fashion and love

- Empower small businesses to scale so they can get out of the rat race and spend more time with loved ones (especially immigrant families)

- Educate others on how to live their healthiest life

- Uncover the potential of the overlooked populations

- Reduce domestic and family violence through education, community and opportunities

- Teach new skills to people who wouldn't otherwise have the opportunity

- Build strong, meaningful communities through sport

Your passion, driver, fire or 'mission' can be anything your heart desires. Just remember that passion shouldn't be the only thing motivating you forward. Many people who only rely on passion for work burn out!

The 'passion tax' is a term coined by Professor Aaron Kay, who led research at Duke University's School of Business in 2019. Across eight studies involving more than 2,400 participants, Kay and his team found a consistent pattern: the more passionate someone is about their work, the more likely they are to be exploited. This held true across industries, roles and participant groups (from students to managers).[19]

---

19 Kay, A., Kim, J., Campbell, T. H., & Shepherd, S. (2019). *Understanding Contemporary Forms of Exploitation: Attributions of Passion Serve to Legitimize the Poor Treatment of Workers.* Journal of Personality and Social Psychology.

'Managers: it's time to stop
taking advantage of enthusiasm.
End the passion tax.'

ADAM GRANT

Under the 'guise' of passion, you may have witnessed, first hand, people you know accept fewer benefits, neglect their health, and accept lower pay and poorer working conditions.

I have, so I use my platforms to advocate against this narrative because it urgently needs to be challenged. We need to recognise that passion is not the only, or even the most sustainable anchor for decision-making. It does help to know what lights you up, what you care for, and maybe that is not through your work, maybe that is through other ways you show up. Even reading this book is an immense privilege. So much of the world is still in survival mode. They don't even think about building their brand.

If you start looking outside your passion and purpose and start looking at ways to articulate what you are and how it fits into the world, the world will return to you. The point of this exercise is to be able to go through life and your career with consistency so that when you are looking for new opportunities, those decisions come easily! If you do this, your confidence will come so much more naturally!

Pairing your passion, your mastery and your superpower is the key to discovering your path forward and developing your personal brand. Not sure what your superpower is yet? Let's figure it out together!

Superpower

The purpose of this is to uncover your natural gifts. What can you do more easily than others? For example, my gift is my ability to develop trusting and warm relationships quickly across all different groups. It is definitely a gift in my toolbox and helps me stand out.

So, what do you think you can do more easily than others? Don't be shy! It's important to name your gifts (your superpowers) for what they are. If you're not entirely sure what your superpower is, then think about what others have told you you're good at. That's a good place to start. Here are some examples of superpowers from clients I have worked with:

- Bringing visions and concepts into reality

- Identifying potential in people and companies

- Calmly navigating ambiguity and uncertainty with good judgement

- Clearly articulating complex information in an accessible and fun way

- Influencing people and shifting their minds to an aligned outcome

- Quickly and accurately assessing a situation (strong intuition)

What are timeless skills?

Not sure what your superpowers are yet? That's completely okay. In the meantime, I always recommend investing in timeless skills – ones that stay relevant no matter your age, industry, or how fast the world is evolving.

Even if you're unclear on what you want to do with your life or feel you've lost your spark, these skills will not only remain valuable but also help you stand out in surprising ways. Whether you're entering the workforce, re-entering it, simply trying to reconnect with your work mojo, or even volunteering for work experience, honing these skills will always be worth it.

One thing I've learnt over the years: *common sense isn't so common.* I would almost label these skills as bare minimum professional skills and attributes. These are the kinds of skills that will serve you, even when AI, nanotech, or flying robots take over. Understanding what these timeless qualities are will help you spot them in yourself, or at the very least begin to grow them. As you read through the list, notice which ones resonate. You might already have more of them than you think.

1   **Problem-solving**: You come up with solutions to problems, not just more problems. This is a great skill to practise and develop as you go through your career, as it helps your managers deal with their mental load.

2   **Accountability**: Work is not everything, and you may not even enjoy your role; however, if you are working for someone, you take pride in what you deliver. When something doesn't go as planned, you take ownership and provide an update with clear next steps.

3   **Critical thinking**: You question assumptions and decisions to find alternative outcomes.

4   **Willingness to learn**: A number of studies of successful executives have highlighted that a lifelong learning mentality is a standout feature. The world is evolving at such a pace that it would be naïve not to see life as a place for ongoing learning.

5   **'A safe pair of hands'**: I developed a strong reputation built on trust; my managers knew if they asked me to do something, I would deliver properly but also use my strong initiative to think five steps ahead. Strong initiative kept stakeholders aware across the work and ensured work was tracked, so anyone could pick up on it if needed. No sneaky motives.

6   **Receptive to feedback**: You can receive and act on feedback without argument or resentment (within reason) and know when to pick your battles.

7   **Positive demeanour**: Our demeanours are very contagious, and if you have a good one, then doors open for you because people will like having you around. The word *energy* is being used in the mainstream, and is good energy commercial? Yes! Have you heard of the airport test? Look it up.

8   **Customer oriented**: Always, always care about your customer, regardless of whether they are internal or external. They are the ones bringing in revenue. Remember, it's not about you; it's about how you are helping to solve their problem.

9   **Meeting preparation and actions**: Time is an important asset, and the amount wasted on meetings with no outcomes is ridiculous. Being conscious of this and efficient in how you operate with something as simple as an agenda and follow-up will help you stand out, and also enable leaders to trust you to deliver the work required.

10 **Give credit where it's due and remember those who helped you**: This is a wonderful leadership practice that anyone can engage in. Acknowledging when others have done the work, even if they're not in the room, says a lot

about you. Even if your work culture doesn't model this yet, your actions can still make a meaningful impact.

11 **Phone-savvy**: With fewer people feeling comfortable talking on the phone, and instead hiding behind text messages and emails, being confident in having phone conversations will make you stand out (even better in person).

12 **Communication**: From how you write an email, present, manage stakeholders and share insights. I know this can be more difficult for some personality types, but the wonderful part is that with generative AI you can get support with this. If you are able to convey what is in your mind on a screen or to a group, it will help you so much!

EXERCISE
YOUR PURSUIT
OF MASTERY

If you're having trouble identifying your mastery, passion or superpower, here are some prompts to help you dig deeper and explore your options. Usually, when I do this with clients, we start with superpowers, as they're easier, and then shift to passion or mastery (depending on which one is more obvious).

SUPERPOWER

- What can you do naturally that usually takes effort for others?

- Is there something you usually receive positive feedback or comments on?

PASSION

- Is there anything that you watch or hear that provides you with an overwhelming sense of clarity or joy, or makes your blood boil with rage?

- What do you like to spend your spare time learning about? Why?

MASTERY

- What professional muscle do you want to continually grow and improve?

- Is there someone you admire for the way they have built their career? Why? What skill did they have that you admire?

P³studio
PEOPLE
PURPOSE
PARTNERSHIPS

4 Unpack your why

Your mastery: your ongoing discipline and craft. It's simple to explain, timeless, and industry and role agnostic (no, you won't always enjoy it, but it's worth the effort as experience pays off!)

Building great places to work: aligned, profitable and sustainable, with a great culture

Your superpowers: your gifts to the world and things you can do more easily than others	**Your passion:** what you care so deeply about that it provides you with an overwhelming sense of fire, clarity or joy
• Building **deep, trusted connections** very quickly across all groups • A commercial mind that understands the **impact of human nuance** on decision-making	• **Reducing domestic violence** – raising awareness, opening economic doors, and creating financial literacy and community • **Reducing the wealth and opportunity gap** by sharing knowledge, connections and opportunities

The pursuit of mastery is a loved framework for deciphering your personal brand. When you are clear on what you are great at, what you want to strive to get better at and what you deeply care about, it will change your demeanour, your decisions and your discussions.

This framework is NOT about comparing. It's about you taking ownership of your story, how you want to partner the great gifts you have been given, and how you want to share them with the world in a way that aligns with what you care about. It will also help you gain a competitive edge in your target market.

> 'Fight for the things that you care about, but do it in a way that will lead others to join you.'

the late **RUTH BADER GINSBURG**
former Associate Justice of the
Supreme Court of the United States

Tall poppy syndrome

Across Australia, New Zealand, Canada, Japan and Scandinavia, there's often a cultural pressure not to stand out too much – a mindset commonly known as *tall poppy syndrome*. It can make people hesitate to share their achievements for fear of seeming arrogant or drawing unwanted attention. Whether your confidence is loud or soft, bold or reflective, your message matters.

We all have moments of self-doubt, especially in a world quick to critique. The fun part is doing it anyway; this is what sets apart those who live fully from those who sit on the sidelines. Expression isn't arrogance; it's courage. And every time you own your story, you give others permission to own theirs too. Besides, when you're focused on building, you don't have time to hate. The ones who criticise? They're just watching from the sidelines. Let them. This is your life, not theirs.

A note on self-doubt and imposter syndrome

It's human to sometimes feel a bit out of place or nervous, especially when trying something new. In my line of work, I see confidence as a big issue. The truth is that we are never going to be 100% at anything, but if you find something that you are great at and deeply care about, then yes, people want to be around that.

According to the Merriam-Webster dictionary, imposter syndrome is a psychological condition characterised by persistent doubt concerning one's abilities or accomplishments, accompanied by the fear of being exposed as a fraud despite evidence of ongoing success.

To some of you, that might be a foreign concept or the first time you have heard such a word – if so, I do deeply applaud you. When imposter syndrome is in the driver's seat, it can quietly limit your potential and keep you from showing up fully; imagine constantly stalling your car while driving up a hill or running a race with your shoelaces tied together. If you do this, you will never go anywhere! The more you recognise your own strengths, the more others will too – and your essence deserves to be seen.

'Don't be afraid to start
small. Every big success
begins with a small step.'

MELANIE PERKINS
co-founder and CEO, Canva

Okay, if you made it through the pursuit of mastery exercise above, then by now you should have a general sense of what you're good at and what you care about in life. The next step is figuring out how those things tie in with your value system.

Your personal values

Values are your set of ethics and principles that govern decisions and set the foundation for the way you operate. They can be an anchor for decision-making, managing biases, determining your criteria for who you work with, and feeding into your brand!

There has been a lot of research on the impact that values have on a company. When I work with organisations, I see values become the anchor point for decision-making for who they hire, retain, promote, partner with and work with. The purpose of values is to remove bias and identify what behaviours and characteristics are important to achieve the goal and larger vision of your company. We know there are lots of companies that do lip service to their values, but the ones that do this well and embed their values across each department stand the test of time. I also see that values make it much less personal and remove the human ego and messiness. And it's based on something bigger; it's aligned with your driver.

- According to LinkedIn's Global Talent Trends Report, 80% of employees say they are more likely to stay with an organisation that has strong values.[20] Furthermore, companies with clear values attract top talent, reducing recruitment costs by 50%.

- Organisations with a strong set of values encourage creativity and innovation, reporting 20% more innovative initiatives and successful product launches, according to the Boston Consulting Group.[21]

A great example of lived values can be found in the charter of the Sydney Gay and Lesbian Mardi Gras, in which you can see the details of their ethical charter and which talks about who they partner with and their criteria for choosing partners. When I was co-hosting a panel, a recent partner shared that they actually check the criteria and have turned down partners who were only interested in 'rainbow washing'. Here are the values they look for in a partner.

- **Diversity, equity and inclusion (DEI)**: We want to partner with industry leaders in diversity, equity and inclusion – who champion DEI as an integral part of their organisation and culture.

20 LinkedIn Talent Solutions. (2022). *Global Talent Trends 2022: The Reinvention of Company Culture*. LinkedIn Corporation. Retrieved from https://business.linkedin.com/content/dam/me/business/en-us/talent-solutions-lodestone/body/pdf/global_talent_trends_2022.pdf.

21 *Boston Consulting Group. (2023). Most Innovative Companies 2023: Reaching New Heights in Uncertain Times*. Retrieved from https://www.bcg.com/publications/2023/advantages-through-innovation-in-uncertain-times.

- **Human rights and sustainability**: We want to partner with organisations with a shared vision of a fair and just world, who share a commitment to human rights and environmental sustainability.

- **Collaboration**: We want to partner with long-standing supporters of our community, who want to stick by us for the years to come, and share a commitment to a strong and transparent partnership.

- **Authenticity and integrity**: We want to partner with organisations that share a deep and authentic commitment to our communities, align with our values, and are genuinely invested in seeing our communities thrive.

So, if companies do this, then why not identify what is important to you? You are already living this subconsciously, so it's time to bring it out in the open!

For example, here are my values for both myself and my company, P3 Studio, and how they show up in my everyday life and influence who I work with:

- **Depth**: warmth, genuine connection to clients, partners and people

- **Respect**: open to other experiences and voices

- **Innovation**: aspiring to do better with a curious, growth mindset

- **Trust**: commit to deliver with high integrity

- **Humour**: a coping mechanism

I cannot stand being around people who only want transactional short-term relationships, in both my network and my friendships. I am the type of person who knows the local café owners and the farmer from whom I buy flowers. I prioritise warmth and connection so much that I travel almost an hour at times to get my nails done because, after four years, I have befriended my nail technician and I want to continue to support her small business.

I also know I dislike being around people and environments filled with victim mentality; accountability and ownership are very important to me, hence innovation. It is also very hard for me to respect and trust someone who has no self-awareness, or is too wrapped up in their ego and insecurities and needs to battle and hurt others to justify their actions. Finally, I use humour as a coping mechanism. I find it hard to connect and build a deeper relationship with anyone who is not able to laugh at life with me (lucky that Australians especially love to laugh).

Now, please be mindful that cultural influences play a role, depending on where you are listening to or reading this. When I was in university studying international business, we learned about Hofstede dimensions, which outline the cultural differences between countries.[22] I also use this framework and the GLOBE study when I work within companies to identify where they sit across the scale and determine where they want to be – a very effective tool for understanding context and implementing change if needed.[23]

You will notice that these differences might influence you. Understanding the differences can help identify why certain values may resonate more than others.

---

22 Hofstede, G. (2001). *Culture's Consequences: Comparing Values, Behaviors, Institutions, and Organizations Across Nations* (2nd ed.). SAGE Publications.

23 House, R. J., Hanges, P. J., Javidan, M., Dorfman, P. W., & Gupta, V. (2004). *Culture, Leadership, and Organizations: The GLOBE Study of 62 Societies.* SAGE Publications.

- **Individualism vs collectivism**: Individualism and collectivism are cultural orientations that shape values and behaviour. Collectivist societies emphasise group harmony, interdependence and shared success, and value loyalty and long-term relationships. In contrast, individualistic societies prioritise personal goals, independence and self-expression, and celebrate individual achievements and autonomy. It is interesting to see how wider factors influence companies depending on their industry. I also see differences with clients from the US and Middle East, versus those in Australia.

- **Power distance**: High power-distance cultures accept hierarchical structures and authority, whereas low power-distance cultures promote equality and upward mobility, and challenge power imbalances. Startups and small businesses often exhibit lower power-distance due to their lean structure, while larger corporations tend to have a higher power-distance.

- **Uncertainty avoidance**: Societies with low uncertainty avoidance embrace ambiguity, change and informal agreements, whereas those with high uncertainty avoidance prefer predictability, strict rules and formal structures. You can see this translate in high-risk work environments such as startups and tech versus highly regulated industries such as finance, insurance and government.

- **Time orientation**: Future-oriented societies, such as Japan and China, focus on long-term goals and perseverance. In contrast, short-term oriented societies, such as the USA and Australia, prioritise immediate results and living in the present. We often see this in organisations, depending on whether their end goal is acquisition or IPO (listing in public).

- **Gender egalitarianism**: Low gender egalitarianism societies uphold traditional gender roles with fewer women in leadership, whereas high gender egalitarianism societies promote gender equality in decision-making, education and the workplace. We often see this translate into workplaces, and it can be a challenge for those who are not used to seeing men or women in certain roles, such as men as nurses or women in engineering, which hinders society in general.

- **Assertiveness**: Highly assertive cultures value competition, direct communication and high performance, where-as less assertive cultures prioritise modesty, co-operation and indirect communication. This is a great reflection; while someone could value honesty and directness, another values modesty.

- **Being vs doing**: Doing-oriented societies focus on productivity, innovation and control, while being-oriented societies emphasise quality of life, harmony and a flexible approach to time. For example, cultural differences in time perception and orderliness can be seen when comparing the Philippines and Germany.

- **Care orientation**: Cultures high in care orientation emphasise compassion, generosity and strong social support systems. In contrast, cultures low in care orientation prioritise independence and self-reliance. For example, in high care-oriented workplaces, leaders may implement flexible policies to support employees through personal hardships, while in low care-oriented cultures, employees are expected to manage such challenges on their own.

- **Indulgence vs restraint**: Indulgent cultures encourage enjoyment, leisure and the open expression of desires, while restrained cultures emphasise self-discipline, control and adherence to social norms. For instance, an indulgent workplace might promote regular celebrations, casual dress codes and work-life balance initiatives. In contrast, a restrained one may uphold formal structures, limit non-work-related activities and expect strict professionalism. You can see this translate across industries. You may not prefer one style over another, but I know I definitely do!

Be mindful of the information above as you go through this exercise, as there might be cultural factors that influence what you find important. I come from an Indian background, which values the collective; however, we grew up with no extended family in an individualistic society, so we developed a strong sense of independence as well. I would say we are in the middle. I definitely see the benefits of both, and don't look at this with judgement but with understanding.

EXERCISE
YOUR VALUES

You may have a sense of what you value. To help you out, here is a list of common values we see.

Step 1: Circle the values that resonate with you. Go first with a word you feel in your body, whether it's a gut feeling or a tinge of excitement.

Step 2: Narrow your list it down to ten, and see if there is anything you can group. Here are some values you can choose from, but feel free to add your own:

Abundance	Decisiveness	Intelligence	Preparedness
Acceptance	Dedication	Intuition	Proactivity
Accountability	Dependability	Joy	Professionalism
Achievement	Depth	Kindness	Punctuality
Adventure	Diversity	Knowledge	Relationships
Advocacy	Empathy	Leadership	Reliability
Ambition	Encouragement	Learning	Resilience
Appreciation	Engagement	Lifelong learning	Resourcefulness
Attractiveness	Enthusiasm	Love	Respect
Autonomy	Ethics	Loyalty	Responsibility
Balance	Excellence	Mindfulness	Responsiveness
Being the best	Expressiveness	Motivation	Security
Benevolence	Fairness	Optimism	Self-control
Boldness	Family	Open-mindedness	Selflessness
Brilliance	Friendships	Originality	Simplicity
Calmness	Flexibility	Passion	Stability
Caring	Freedom	Performance	Success
Challenge	Fun	Personal development	Teamwork
Charity	Generosity	Proactive	Thankfulness
Cheerfulness	Grace	Professionalism	Thoughtfulness
Cleverness	Growth	Quality	Traditionalism
Community	Flexibility	Recognition	Trustworthiness
Communication	Happiness	Risk taking	Understanding
Commitment	Health	Safety	Uniqueness
Compassion	Honesty	Security	Usefulness
Cooperation	Humility	Service	Versatility
Collaboration	Humour	Spirituality	Vision
Consistency	Impact	Stability	Warmth
Contribution	Inclusiveness	Peace	Wealth
Creativity	Independence	Perfection	Well-being
Credibility	Individuality	Playfulness	Wisdom
Curiosity	Innovation	Popularity	Zeal
Daring	Inspiration	Power	

Step 3: Once you have selected your values, here are some nudging questions:

- Are there certain qualities you admire about someone? Why? Reflect back on those you admired and/or memorable mentors.

- Has there ever been a time when you had to walk away from a personal or professional relationship? Why? Reflect on your last few roles.

- What is something you cannot stand in other people?

- What is something that you find really important in another person (e.g., friend, colleague)?

- Are there certain qualities in a person that take precedence over others?

By now you should have four or five values that deeply resonate with you, that you can articulate within your business and even scout for when looking for new partners, employees or employers. Articulating your values becomes a great tool to help with decision-making in all parts of your life. You can even share your values with your future employers; this does help you stand out in interviews, especially if the values align with your prospective employer.

There's one last thing you need to consider as we unpack your briefcase for success, and that's what environments you thrive in best. Understanding your human needs is an important part of growing in both your professional and your personal life.

Environments for growth

Your environment is so much stronger than you realise. This goes especially for your work. For those who can choose and reflect on their workplaces, I implore you to explore the environments where you truly thrive. It's important to balance this with the stage of life you are in.

There is a lot of romanticism about having your own business, and the truth is that it's hard and not everyone is designed to be a business owner or even a leader, and that is completely okay. You can still build a brand that puts you in the driver's seat of decision-making.

Understanding your human needs

At different stages in our lives, we tend to focus on different wants and needs. For example, when we are younger, we tend to choose experiences over ego or money. My therapist introduced me to the six human needs: Certainty, Variety, Significance, Connection, Growth and Contribution, which I use both personally and professionally. This framework was co-created by Chloé Madanes and Tony Robbins,[24] and inspired by Maslow's Hierarchy of Needs. So, what does it mean and how can I relate it to my personal brand and what I look for at work?

CERTAINTY: The need for safety, security, stability, predictability and comfort. We want to feel safe, in control, certain of ourselves and familiar with our environment; predictability is important. You want to be as certain as possible that things will work out the way they are planned and that

---

24 Madanes, C. (n.d.). *The 6 Human Needs*. Madanes Institute. Retrieved from https://madanesinstitute.com/the-6-human-needs/.

people will do as expected. The degree to which certainty is needed or desired, however, varies from person to person.

> How does this show up at work? Examples include a role that involves doing the same tasks every day, where there is little to no change. For some people, having a consistent job in a large, profitable company is important so they can pay their bills and have the predictability that let's them focus on other parts of their life. This can also be applied to romantic settings. My challenge is that now we are in the Fourth Industrial Revolution, there will be a big shift in how we work. If you heavily rely on job certainty, it would be worth learning how your job may evolve and how you can continue to be a valuable member of the team – your wisdom is invaluable.

VARIETY/UNCERTAINTY: The need to feel challenged, to experience change and excitement, to take risks, to be surprised and entertained in our lives. The person caught in the same routine day after day will seek change and look for uncertainty. Just as a sense of security is reassuring, the excitement that comes from variety is necessary to feel alive. For some, variety may be satisfied by watching the news or reality TV, as this is something different from their own life. Others may seek more high-risk activities, such as extreme sports, to satisfy the need for uncertainty. For many, a major source of variety is to experience different kinds of problems.

> How does this show up in work? This need can be met by project-based consulting roles, where there is lots of change and different experiences. This is something I look for personally in my own business. If I don't have variety

and different tasks in what I am working on, then I will become demotivated. This is often the case for small businesses, especially when they start. The variety is exciting as they are wearing many different hats. I do see people sacrifice this need if there is something more important that takes precedence.

SIGNIFICANCE: The need to feel wanted, respected, needed, special and important, and to achieve. Every person has this desire. We can feel significant because we have achieved something, built something or succeeded at something. If you are deeply insecure and seek this validation purely from external sources, then you might be prone to seeking significance by tearing down someone or by people pleasing.

How does this show up at work? How important are you at work? How much does your role influence the work being produced? During the pandemic, people who resonated deeply with this need were challenged when they were no longer able to go to work and get that sense of significance. As people are looking for roles, there is a trend in looking to find meaning in paid work. Other people meet this need by taking up leadership and other roles in the community, such as sports team captains, religious leaders or becoming a parent. My significance comes from the work I do with my drivers, from speaking to facilitating and even from this book.

CONNECTION/LOVE: Everybody strives for a level of connection and affiliation with people around them and wants to feel part of a larger community. We have a need to feel love, togetherness, passion, unity, warmth and desire, which is important to keep our hormone squad happy. The need for love and connection is based on blending in and wanting to belong and be similar to others in a group. Many leaders feel a conflict in that they want to be part of the team, but they must also know when to take charge of the group and make tough decisions.

> How does this show up at work? Feeling as if we belong is incredibly important for survival and hard-wired into our brain, so as times continually change, and we delay having families and relocate for opportunities, there is a sense that work can become a place to seek our community. When I relocated interstate, this was particularly important for me. As I became more established, this became less so. Someone who finds this important will tend to hold back on feedback, and perform above their peers at the risk of not having this need met. It's important to frame how you give feedback and ensure that a recipient's core need won't be compromised. For some people, these dynamics work; for others, it can be quite toxic.

GROWTH: How we are developing, learning, strengthening, cultivating and expanding ourselves. We grow and change emotionally with every experience, and we grow intellectually as we respond to events and the world around us. Some people satisfy the need to grow by working out physically or by reading books. Others need to study and learn constantly to feel that they are truly growing.

> How does this show up at work? This one is really big for the work I do. I stretch myself with my work, constantly learning something new and challenging my own assumptions. If I am not growing at work, then I am stifled and truly the worst version of myself (hence I have my own

business). This is also likely to resonate with people who are highly ambitious in their careers (we will refer to rock vs rocket later). We also see this resonate for people early in their careers, who eagerly seek to absorb new information after school or studies or a break, and for those who are re-entering the workforce. If someone is oriented this way, then make sure you consider them for stretch projects so they are continually expanding. Succession planning can help; otherwise, you could lose a really great talent who wants to help your company grow. As someone who is in this space, I know that you can also leverage your brand and showcase your learnings to the wider community to expand your reach.

CONTRIBUTION: There is a human need to feel we are giving, donating, serving, offering and helping others. To go beyond our own needs and to give to others. A life is incomplete without the sense that one is making a contribution to others or to a cause.

In the workplace, this need for contribution often shows up in different ways. I've observed many people stepping into mentoring or leadership roles, where they help guide others and share their expertise. For some, contribution is expressed through philanthropic efforts, while for me it comes through speaking engagements and keynotes. It's important to understand that contribution isn't just about fulfilling the basic requirements of a job. It's about the deeper meaning, whether that is through work or other means. Many individuals contribute by leading initiatives that align with their company's values. For example, someone might lead an LGBTIQ+ initiative or oversee a Reconciliation Action Plan.

Madanes suggests that our daily decisions and actions are motivated by whichever of the six needs is most predominant in our lives at any given time. As you move along with your life responsibilities, certainty becomes more important and you may sacrifice growth opportunities, or you may get your other needs met elsewhere so your workplace shows up differently for you, and there is *nothing* wrong in this.

For example, right now my key drivers for work are growth and variety; my other needs for connection are met by my incredible circle of friends, family and colleagues, and my speaking engagements fill my need for significance and contribution. The purpose of understanding your human needs is to make work work for you, and to determine if your other needs can be met elsewhere. It gives a realistic view of pursuing the trifecta of superpower, mastery and driver.

In the next section, we will discuss the power of the factors to look for in your old job to help you determine the environments where you thrive. It is good to reflect back and forth as you determine which stage of your life you are in; you will ascertain the environments you enjoy.

Reflecting on the stage you are at with work

There are two terms I use often when I work with clients on their talent, understanding where people are at, and designing future roles. It's important to recognise where you are mentally, based on your human needs and experience at the time. I call the two core work modes 'rock mode' and 'rocket mode'.

Rocket mode: Looking to launch their career, rockets are actively seeking career and growth opportunities, tend to have strong initiative, and work very hard so they can be compensated and promoted in proportion to the work they put in. Rockets tend to get frustrated when there are too many layers. More positively, they are very focused on growing within the company, or externally if they do not get what they want.

Rock mode: Rocks are steady, they provide mentorship, consistency and support to the team, as they have focuses outside the workplace (family, sports, new home, wedding, etc.), or they come to work for the community and connection element. They tend to stay in the same role for a longer period and are not as interested in promotions (they might be financially okay or completely dependent on the job). However, they still do the work required – this is not to promote laziness. Rocks are so incredibly important in an organisation.

It is completely okay to acknowledge the mode that suits you at the time and to be aware of the setup for the role – a job which doesn't have many leadership opportunities may be suited to rocks. At the same time, a small, fast-growing company requires rockets to take on more responsibility and rapidly grow their potential.

Please know there is no shame or judgement either way. When I started my career, I was in rock mode as I was focused on processing the grief of losing my father, getting over being dumped by the person I thought I was going to marry (another story for another day), and being there for my family – yet I was still promoted. When I moved to London, I was more in rock mode (I was busy rocketing across Europe). Then, when I arrived back in Australia, my boss in a global company saw my potential, my career took a complete turn, and I have been in rocket mode since.

I'm giving you this permission to acknowledge quietly or loudly where you are at, and there is nothing wrong with whichever phase you are in. Even rocks can build their personal brand; it's not only for rockets.

EXERCISE
MY HUMAN NEEDS
WITH WORK

- The reason I go to work is to _____

- Work for me is a place I _____

- When there are potential changes in my job,
  I feel very _____

- My colleagues are _____

- An industry/topic I am really curious about is _____

- In terms of my job now, am I in rock or rocket mode?
  Does my work allow me to operate in that mode? Am I
  happy with that, or do I want that to change?

In conclusion, you don't need to reinvent yourself to have a powerful personal brand – you just need to realign with what's already within you.

By now you've clarified your strengths, reconnected with your values and started defining your signature style. Your briefcase is no longer a jumble of 'shoulds' and 'maybes' – it's becoming a toolkit filled with intention.

In the next chapter, we'll explore what it looks like to walk with your briefcase – to live out your values in the way you speak, lead, partner and show up for others.

You have done the digging. Now let's step into the world and carry your briefcase with purpose.

CHAPTER SUMMARY

- **Pursuit of mastery:** When we identify how to commercialise our superpowers (our natural gifts), with our mastery and what we care about, it becomes so much easier to discern our time. Have you figured out what your superpower, mastery and passion are?

- **Expert/imposter syndrome:** What is your relationship with these words? Be aware, but don't let them in the driver's seat; otherwise, life will pass you by.

- **Core values:** Companies know their values, so why wouldn't you? Identifying your core values to anchor and filter your decision-making is such a helpful way to think about things.

- **Human needs:** Identifying where you are in life is so important; how are your human needs currently being met?

REFLECTION QUESTIONS

- What are the timeless skills that set you apart, and how do they show up in your daily work or life?

- When have you felt the most in alignment with your strengths, and what conditions allowed that to happen?

- What limiting beliefs, such as self-doubt or imposter syndrome, hold you back from fully embracing your personal brand/your essence?

- How can you design an environment that supports your growth and allows you to thrive both professionally and personally?

CHAPTER 3

CARRY

Alone we can do so little;
together we can do so much.

HELEN KELLER
author, political activist & lecturer

WHEN DESIGNING the name of my company, P3 Studio, I asked myself: What is most important to me? As a small business owner, my partnership with the commercial world is at the core of everything I do. How do I commercialise my essence while staying true to my values? Your personal brand is a partnership between yourself and the wider world.

P3 Studio stands for People, Purpose and Partnerships – partnering with people to deliver on your purpose. That's what my company is built on. To believe we don't need people at all is to deny the very essence of our humanity. Unlike most species, humans have the longest vulnerability period in early life. We might not have survived if we weren't so endearing as babies. A child is dependent on others for survival, reinforcing the idea that everything in life is, at its core, a partnership.

I recently received praise for my warm, collaborative approach during a negotiation course. When asked if this was my natural style, I paused to reflect. Everything you do is a partnership. When you are in the driver's seat, you can choose how to invest and manage these relationships.

So, I ask you: As you build your personal brand, what partnership are you creating with your own experiences, knowledge and network? Who do you want to align with as you navigate the world?

You've unpacked your briefcase. You've defined your strengths, values, and the things that matter most. Now comes the part that separates intention from impact: how you carry it.

The most aligned personal brands don't live in documents – they live in how you walk through the world, how you respond under pressure, how you partner with others, how you choose to show up even when no one is watching.

In this chapter, we're going to explore what it looks like to live your personal brand through your partnerships, your mindset, and the inner dialogue you carry every day. You'll learn practical tools to put your brand into action, such as the 'quarterly life audit', a step-by-step approach to navigating emotional triggers, and how to become someone whose presence builds trust. Evolving is part of life, so this is about progress, not perfection.

Here's what we will be exploring in this chapter:

- We'll talk about the power of partnerships and how you can harness them for success.

- Then we'll talk about how you show up in your partnerships; your presence matters!

- Next we'll dive into your behaviour patterns and how you can start being more intentional about them, using everything you've learned about your personal brand so far.

The power of partnerships

Partnerships aren't about a transactional 'give and take'. A partnership is a relationship between two or more parties collaborating to achieve shared goals. Similar to networking, partnerships thrive on aligned values and goals – not only in business but also in your personal life. Who you associate with directly impacts your personal brand. Effective partnerships can:

- Increase efficiency by sharing resources
- Drive product innovation and development
- Fast-track credibility and trust
- Provide access to new markets
- Share risk

You, too, can create meaningful partnerships in both personal and professional spaces. Those who excel in personal branding are the ones who build deep, authentic relationships. With the rise of entrepreneurship, smaller businesses and the gig economy, you can cultivate partnerships that elevate your brand. Some are born into influential networks, making partnerships more accessible. But regardless of where you start, effective partnerships require mutual value alignment.

For those who don't have an established network, building relationships takes time and effort. Being deliberate about who you surround yourself with is crucial, not just for opportunities, but for your own well-being.

I learned this lesson the hard way. I've let people into my network too quickly, ignoring red flags, and paid the price. I've fallen for charm without doing my due diligence. But moving forward, I've learned that trust-building takes time, and partnerships should be cultivated with intention.

I had someone email me once after a business group call that I had joined. While I appreciated the hustle, there was no warmth or personalisation to her email. She was asking for referrals. When you ask people for something, remember how important trust is, and remember that your reputation is on the line when you refer people.

Because of the close partnerships I have developed, I have been able to:

- Work internationally

- Receive invitations to exclusive gatherings

- Maintain a strong pulse on market trends through knowledge-sharing

- Secure fantastic clients

- Build credibility and trust across corporate, SMB and startup spaces

- Book speaking engagements

- Elevate the voices of women of colour

- Receive free media exposure

Beyond traditional business networks, I've partnered with consultants in completely different fields, from product development and marketing professionals to finance and tech conference organisers. Partnerships go beyond networking; they offer a chance to co-share your brand, community and resources to create a collective impact.

Your personal brand is not built in isolation. It is shaped by the people, businesses and communities you align with. Be intentional. Be strategic. And most importantly, choose partnerships that reflect your values and aspirations. Below, we will explore how you think about your partnerships.

'If people like you they'll listen
to you, but if they trust you
they'll do business with you.'

the late **ZIG ZIGLAR**
founder of Zig Ziglar Corporation,
author, speaker

Measuring the value of partnerships

How do you quantify the value of a partnership? While return on investment isn't always tangible, there are ways to showcase commercial impact. To get your brain juices flowing, here are some factors to consider:

- Collaborate across departments (including finance teams) to compare costs of media and PR to partnership-driven exposure.

- Analyse post-campaign results in terms of uptake – trusted partnerships open doors faster than traditional marketing efforts (which have identified cost savings).

- Consider the power of talk triggers[25] – when people organically share your brand, they increase visibility and credibility. Studies indicate that 86% of B2B (business to

---

25 Baer, J., & Lemin, D. (2018). *Talk Triggers: The Complete Guide to Creating Customers with Word of Mouth*. Portfolio.

business) purchasing decision makers consider word of mouth (WOM) from peers the most influential source of information and over 80% of B2B buyers share information from the seller with other purchasing decision makers.[26, 27]

EXERCISE
HOW TO SELECT
PARTNERSHIPS

Here are some guidelines to help you think about who to partner with as you build your brand. You can also use these questions to guide you on who to hire, what friendships to build or what training opportunities to pursue. Here's some food for thought:

- **Shared goals & values:** Do they align with what you stand for? What is their moral compass? Do they act with integrity even when no one is watching?

- **Audience overlap:** Are your target markets complementary? Does this partnership add value to both parties' existing audiences?

- **Complementary offerings:** Do your services enhance one another rather than compete? Strong partnerships can create additional value for clients and customers alike.

26 Industrial Marketing Management, 'How B2B firms leverage digital content marketing capabilities for word-of-mouth,' *Industrial Marketing Management*, Volume 112, 2023, Pages 190-204, https://doi.org/10.1016/j.indmarman.2023.05.012. Available at: ScienceDirect.

27 Kumar, V., & Pansari, A. (2023). How B2B firms leverage digital content marketing capabilities for word-of-mouth. *Industrial Marketing Management*, 112, 190–204. https://doi.org/10.1016/j.indmarman.2023.05.012:contentReference{index=0}.

- **Brand alignment:** Are their values, messaging and market presence in sync with yours? Do they treat people with respect, and do they practise critical thinking?

- **Communication & collaboration:** Do they work through challenges effectively? Are they accountable? Do they align internally before engaging externally? Internal mis-alignment can create unnecessary friction and politics in partnerships.

- **Resource sharing:** Is the effort distributed fairly? Are both parties investing equally in the collaboration? It can be disheartening to constantly refer business to a partner and receive nothing in return.

- **Exit strategy & conflict resolution:** Do you have a plan if things do not work out? Is there a clear conflict res-olution process in place to handle misunderstandings professionally?

How to start partnering with intention

I unknowingly practised partnership-building throughout my life, a technique many successful businesses use today. I view all my commercial engagements as partnerships, and integrity is paramount before I exchange money. If you adopt this mindset in all interactions, watch how it will nat-urally strengthen your partnership muscle.

'We sometimes encounter people, even perfect strangers, who begin to interest us at first sight, somehow suddenly, all at once, before a word has been spoken.'

FYODOR MIKHAILOVICH DOSTOEVSKY
author

For instance, my mortgage broker attended my apartment blessing and kitchen renovation party. He later connected with my financial adviser (who also cares about empowering women), and now they're friends. When you truly connect with people, they will likely introduce you to others who share their values. I was surprised to learn that many people don't cultivate these relationships. But for me, it's intentional. I need to believe in the person I work with. Trust is one of my core values, and supporting small businesses aligns with that. Investing in people goes beyond monetary benefits – it creates a rich, interconnected life filled with trust and opportunity. So, choose wisely, and your partnerships will define your journey.

How to write a 'work with me' one-pager

A great way to set the tone and work with new people is to share your preferred ways of working. Please note, this is not an excuse to avoid being adaptive but rather a way to ensure smoother communication and productivity.

When I was an executive assistant to CEOs and leader-ship teams or working on large projects, I would ask questions to understand preferences better. For example, I needed to know whether they preferred phone calls, text messages or emails. Did they like to discuss things verbally, or were they more comfortable with written communication? How spontaneous were they, and did they need review times for documents? This insight helped me function effectively as their right-hand person and ensured we were operating as a well-functioning team. It is important to ask what operating systems they prefer too (I am an Apple and Google person, but I know many companies use other collaboration tools).

As you progress in your career and take on more senior roles, it becomes increasingly important to communicate your preferences. Depending on your culture and ways of working, this can be distributed to those you work with closely or shared in the company drive. Creating a one-pager doesn't need to be overwhelming. If you've done the work from previous chapters, you can easily put some prompts into a large language model (generative AI) to help you articulate your best practices.

Some people may choose to include personal details. For instance, I would note the anniversary date of my father's passing as a non-negotiable day that I take off. By providing this level of transparency, you're setting clear expectations, which leads to more effective and harmonious interactions and getting work done.

EXAMPLE
'HOW TO WORK WITH ME' ONE-PAGER

Here is an example of a one-pager completed by one of my clients, to give you a better of idea of what it can look like.

BEST WAYS TO WORK WITH ME

- **Give space for reflection:** Allow me time to process ideas independently before expecting detailed feedback or decisions.

- **Encourage early sharing:** Ask questions to help me vocalise and refine ideas, and provide further input as your views change, even if they feel incomplete.

- **Communication:** I prefer phone calls to emails, so if it's urgent, please call or text.

- **Collaborate strategically:** Pair me with individuals who excel in execution and detail-oriented tasks to complement my creative big ideas.

- **Focus on big-picture discussions:** I am a forward thinker, so engage me in conversations about strategy, innovation and long-term goals.

- **Be open to exploration:** I thrive in environments where new approaches and creative problem-solving are welcomed.

MY STRENGTHS

- **Innovative thinker:** I excel at generating out-of-the-box ideas.

- **Objective problem-solver:** I create structured criteria to assess situations and find new solutions.

- **Open-minded:** I value diverse perspectives and am receptive to unconventional approaches.

- **Data-driven decision-making:** I make informed decisions based on thorough analysis and evidence, plotting a path that provides optionality as ideas are implemented.

- **Reliable, trustworthy and calm:** I maintain confidentiality and provide a consistent, calming presence among business chaos.

WHAT WILL NOT BE HELPFUL

- **Rushing decisions:** Pressure to finalise ideas with inadequate time for reflection or testing can lead to less-than-ideal outcomes.

- **Overlooking timelines:** While I value thorough research, reminders to balance exploration with practical deadlines are critical, so give me timelines and milestones.

- **Dismissing the process:** Only focusing on action and execution, without engaging in strategic discussions or listening to other perspectives, is a demotivating factor for me.

- **Bureaucratic constraints:** Excessive red tape or rigid structures will hinder my ability to innovate and add value.

- **Assuming understanding:** My thought processes may not always be obvious; encouraging me to share with an open mind and explain the rationale will help align outcomes.

The friendship audit

Have you ever done a friendship or social audit before? This concept may seem more aligned with personal relationships, but I believe there's a strong connection between your friendships and how you show up in the commercial world. How you cultivate and maintain relationships in your personal life can directly impact your professional life.

For example, consider applying your friendship dynamics to your business relationships. Personally, I find that my 'secret sauce' is surrounding myself with people who are low maintenance but high return – those who add value to my life without draining me or requiring much maintenance, who completely understand nuance and don't take things personally (in other words, they're really fun to be around, but I also know they have my back).

Take a moment to reflect on the people you surround yourself with – both personally and professionally. When was the last time you considered the quality of these relationships? You may remember quizzes like this from *DOLLY* magazine (I'm showing my age here), but now it's time to practise this as you navigate your life. Over time, as you level up, you'll find yourself doing this naturally in all areas of your life.

The friendship audit scoresheet
Answer the bold question and use the other questions to help determine your rating (1 = low, 5 = high).

QUESTIONS	RATING (1–5)
How do I feel when I'm around them? How do I feel when I see their name pop up on my phone?	
Do they bring out the best or the worst in me? Do I leave feeling drained or uplifted?	
How do they handle life's tough moments? Do they tackle challenges or spiral into victimhood?	
How often is the conversation about them? Do they ask about me? Do they care, or am I just a convenient listening ear? Do they take advantage of my goodwill?	
Do they make an effort to connect with me? Do they show up for important events or occasions?	
Do I matter to them? (Do they celebrate my success?) When I am going through tough or great times, do they show up for me? Likewise, do they matter to me?	
Do we respect each other? Do I value their opinion? Disagreements are natural, but being around people you don't respect is hard.	
How strong is their moral compass? What is in their internal default setting? How do they act when no one is watching? Do I trust them?	
Does time apart make a difference in our interactions?	
If my status changed (marital status, job, location), would it impact how they treat me? In other words, are they in my orbit for who I am or for what I can offer them?	

Now, if you do ratings with your friends, please note that these change over time depending on your life stage. Here's how I suggest ranking your partnerships, based on the total score they received from the chart above.

10–20: Community & acquaintances

These individuals are part of your broader network. It's important to recognise that your 'weak ties' connect you to networks outside your own circle, which can be crucial for unlocking opportunities.[28] A great paper, *Strength of Weak Ties* by Mark Granovetter, dives into this concept. So, while you may not rely on them for major personal moments, don't disregard this group. Be mindful of the role they play in your life, and recognise that the relationship may evolve if your, or even their status changes.

20–30: Curated connections

These people are peripheral figures in your life – usually connected through extracurricular activities or work. You'll likely share group experiences and have light-hearted conversations with them, but the connection is more casual.

30–40: Core circle

These are your emotional support system. There is deep trust, and you tend to invest in one-on-one quality time with them. You share common values, and they are the ones you turn to in moments of vulnerability.

40–50: Chosen family

These individuals remain present throughout your life, and you invest in these relationships because their influence meaningfully contributes to your personal development and well-being. You trust them with your perspective, and their support provides stability and clarity during periods of change.

---

28 Granovetter, M. S. (1973). The strength of weak ties. *American Journal of Sociology*, 78(6), 1360–1380. https://doi.org/10.1086/22546.

Was there anyone who surprised you once you did the audit? Your life partners (including your friends, business partners, colleagues, family, and more) should be a source of inspiration and joy, and you should bring out the best in each other.

'It's a long, long road. Sometimes all you need are people who pat your back and say, carry on. Thank you to everyone who encourages.'

SHARADDHA SHARMA
founder of Yourstory

Quarterly life audit

As Socrates said, 'The unexamined life is not worth living.' This is an activity I do with one of my dearest friends, who is a sister to me – coincidentally, her name is Venesha as well (yes, really!). I want to emphasise the value of doing this exercise with someone else, as it brings a sense of account-ability and reflection. We do an annual check-in, setting three overarching goals for the year and six key factors to measure ourselves against.

Here's how we approach our session (feel free to adapt this to what works for you; you can draw questions from the alignment check that we did in Chapter 1):

- **Frequency**: Quarterly, in a fun setting, such as between hikes, adventures or other enjoyable activities.

- **Approach**: Either prepare beforehand or do the activity together in real time.

- **Reflect on the past three months:** Evaluate your current situation based on the following six factors (feel free to tailor these categories to your own life).

  - Financial/wealth
  - Career/work
  - Love/relationships
  - Living situation/environment
  - Health (mental, emotional, physical)
  - Social/family/friends/community

- **Share reflections:** Listen to one another – it's an exchange!

- **Celebrate achievements:** Acknowledge the positive steps taken and milestones reached.

- **Set goals for the next three months:** Establish new goals for the upcoming quarter that you'll review at your next catch-up.

- **Final step:** Embrace accountability by assessing your progress against your overarching yearly goals (typically, people aspire to three major goals: career, relationship and home).

Remember your personal brand and essence walk with you every day – the more aligned you are with how you want to live, the easier your briefcase will be to carry.

Showing up with intention

Why do two people experience the same event, yet walk away with wildly different stories? We often see this in business when there are mass layoffs. Some people leave the company, shooting off into the next opportunity, while others take the change much harder. I've been brought into companies experiencing redundancy to facilitate sessions to help navigate these moments – not with false hope or forced optimism, but with frameworks that honour both the grief of change and the power of agency.

The trick? It was about acknowledging that setbacks are tough and providing practical strategies and frameworks for moving forward. I've led this exercise in quite a few organisations, and it's all about taking radical responsibility for how we process things. Trust me, it all helps with personal branding. It's about showing up for yourself and others and addressing your mindset.

People are fascinating. Life, as we know it, is filled with uncertainty and hardships. However, how people react and overcome these challenges varies greatly. Why is it that some people seem to process difficult situations with a growth mindset, while others are more fixed in their responses? The answer lies in Carol Dweck's research about mindset. Sometimes, it's easy to spot someone going through a hard time, especially when angry or visibly upset.

When I feel overwhelmed, I've learnt to ask: Who's speaking in my mind right now? Is it fear? Old programming? Or something wiser? I call these parts my 'residents' – and I've come to know them well. Understanding them doesn't mean I don't react; it means I choose how I respond.

Today, we'll explore what happens in those critical milliseconds between a trigger and your response.

Neuroscience tells us the amygdala – our emotional smoke alarm – fires up when we feel threatened, even by an email or silence. But not every loud internal alarm is telling the truth.[29] Today, you'll meet your own residents, get to know their patterns, and begin to choose which ones you'd like to drive your decisions. You will be your best-case study.

Disclaimer: This is deep, personal work. The purpose is not to make you change overnight but to help you understand the stories you've inherited, so you can decide which ones to keep and which ones to rewrite. Because while we can't control the chaos, we *can* choose how we show up.

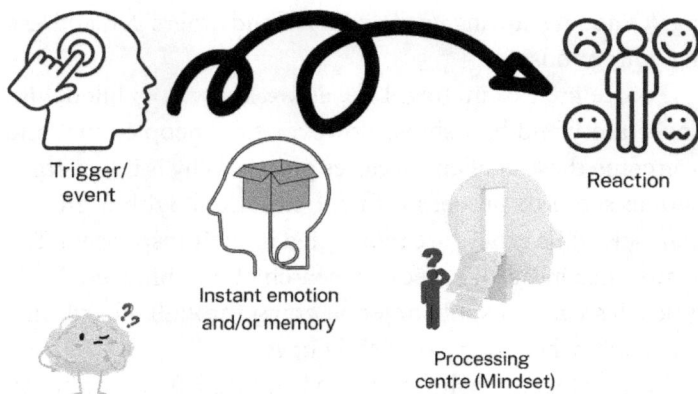

Trigger/event

Instant emotion and/or memory

Processing centre (Mindset)

Reaction

Mindset – from trigger to reaction

---

29 LeDoux, J. (2015). *Anxious: Using the brain to understand and treat fear and anxiety.* Viking.

Who runs the household of your mind?

I love this concept, which I heard years ago from a monk named Sharon Salzberg. She explains that much of our suffering comes from forgetting that *we* run the household – that our mind is our home (whether you call it your essence, soul, heart, mindset, or something else).

Sharon shares that certain emotions come knocking on the door when an event or trigger occurs. In that moment, we have two choices:

1 **Welcome them in as guests** and listen to what they have to say.

2 **Shut the door**, only for them to force their way in through air vents or windows, causing chaos and taking over the space.

I became curious and began building on the idea. Once emotions knock on the door, *who* welcomes them in? The goal is to become aware of why you react the way you do and have fun figuring out your 'roommates'. Here's an example of how this can play out in real life:

Example 1:
- **Trigger**: You enter a store or discussion and feel overlooked.

- **Memory**: Being ignored at school or at home.

- **Feelings**: Loneliness, unworthiness and self-pity knock on the door.

- **Reaction**: Do you shift your perspective or spiral?

Example 2:
- **Trigger**: You miss out on a grant, opportunity or funding.

- **Memory**: A teacher or parent once told you your ideas were stupid.

- **Feelings**: Self-doubt and imposter syndrome knock on the door.

- **Reaction**: Do you self-sabotage or see this as a chance to learn and separate your worth from your achievements?

Example 3:
- **Trigger**: Someone cuts you off in traffic.

- **Memory**: Moments when you felt disrespected or times when people dismissed your needs or boundaries.

- **Feelings**: Anger and fear knock on the door.

- **Reaction**: Do you road rage or practise empathy and depersonalisation – assume positive intent (API)?

Now imagine that after the feeling arrives – whichever form it takes – it knocks on the door. Who is welcoming them in? Who are the visitors, the roommates and the regulars living in your mind and driving your reaction?

You get the idea. Now, remember that this entire process happens in milliseconds. That's why people often say, 'Take a deep breath,' when something overwhelming happens – it gives you a moment to pause and regain control. This is also why the same event can trigger completely different reactions in different people. I had a client who was in an abusive marriage for twenty years. When she felt ignored at networking events, it would trigger her hypervigilance, and it blocked her from developing great business relationships. Our body creates mechanisms to protect us, so it's not about judging but being aware of its impact.

The goal here is not just self-awareness, but understanding your default ways of coping and thinking (this is not easy work) because they impact everything – how you write, handle feedback, and show up in relationships, networking events and work.

Meet the roomies, regulars and visitors

Simplifying the concept of a growth mindset into tangible characters can be a fun and meaningful way to explore which mental residents are helping you and which ones may need to be evicted.

For example, my house is occupied by acceptance, gratitude, a jester, compassion/empathy, adventure, optimism, curiosity and intellect. Together, they provide me with perspective, reason and resilience (and keep me in the intentional driver's seat). Below, I will share a bit more about my roommates and the practical role they play in how I show up and respond to the world.

- **Acceptance**: Always the first to open the door. Ever heard people say, 'I can't believe this happened!?' The first step to processing anything is to accept that it *did* happen. Acceptance helps me decide how to move forward and which roommates I need to call to have tea with my emotions.

- **Empathy and compassion:** Empathy is feeling another person's emotions. Compassion is being mindful of suffering, without ignoring it, running from it or becoming overwhelmed by it. These help me remove my ego and see how I can show up for others, recognising that sometimes people don't need solutions; they just need someone to sit with them in their pain.

- **Gratitude**: A huge role-player that keeps me from spiralling into victim mode. Gratitude reminds me of the goodness in my life and connects me to something larger – whether that's other people, nature or a higher power. This roommate always reminds me of how hard I worked to get where I am and to be grateful for all I've achieved, instead of always looking at how much more I need to do. (Because there will *always* be more to do).

- **Jester**: An archetype that is at peace with the paradoxes of the world. He uses humour to illuminate hypocrisy. The jester is a fun-loving character who seeks the now, inviting others to partake in creating a self-deprecating form of satire. The jester keeps me grounded, reminding me not to take myself seriously, helps to keep me light-hearted and playful, and brings in humour, even among the most painful and heaviest emotions.

Let's apply this to a real-world scenario so you understand how we can choose which part of us shows up to respond in this world, especially when we're faced with adversity.

Depersonalisation has been a game-changer for me. It's the practice of removing yourself from the equation and realising everyone is dealing with their struggles. If someone is rude, it's likely a reflection of what's going on in their mind, not a personal attack. *In essence, not everything is about you!* I thank my human behaviour coach for instilling this in me!

Hurt people hurt people. Empowered people empower people. It is that simple. If we could all recognise that everyone is fighting their own unseen battles, the world would be a little kinder – and we need kindness more than ever.

You see, my friend, when you operate from a place of true love and understanding, it naturally becomes part of your personal brand because you live, breathe and feel it.

Your turn: Who's living in your mind?

Because life will always be filled with pain, the question is: How do you want to show up for it? Now, take a moment to reflect. What housemates and roomies are taking residence in your mind? And remember – you can always change them if you do the work.

Now let's explore your own mind-household. When emotions come knocking, which roommates do you have greeting them? Which ones need to be called on more often? And which ones might be overstaying their welcome?'

EXERCISE
WHO LIVES IN
YOUR MIND?

What emotion or memory comes up for you when you are triggered? Write down some examples of your triggers. What memories are attached to them? Feel free to mind-map this as you journal to keep your thoughts flowing. Emotions and triggers are often non-linear, so allow yourself to explore.

Who are the roommates attached to these emotions? Who is welcoming each trigger at the door? Consider some of the following to determine who lives rent-free inside your head.

Gratitude	Acceptance	Resentment
Fear	Denial	Problem-solver
Risk taker	Anger	Optimism
Humility	Anxiety	Pessimism
Compassion	Jealousy	Victim
Self-belief	Adventurer	Entitlement
Jester	Pride	Insecurity
Hope	Disgust	Love

**NEXT, PICK A TRIGGER SITUATION
(HERE ARE SOME SUGGESTIONS):**
- When someone cuts you off in traffic
- When you receive feedback from work/peers
- Passive aggression or avoidance from a friend

LET'S WORK THROUGH IT TOGETHER:

- What is your usual reaction to this situation? Which emotion is knocking at your door?
- Who is welcoming them in?
- Is there an ideal way you would like to react in the moment? Which roommate would you like to welcome this trigger in versus who actually is?

Repeat this part with as many scenarios as you like.

As you analyse how you react to each trigger, you might notice how your responses may lean more towards positive or negative. As I mentioned, how you respond to triggers (and your emotions) defines how you show up in the world. This can greatly affect your growth as a human and has an impact on your personal brand. Doing the work to show up how you want others to see you (your ideal brand) is about changing our mindsets and behaviour in the moment. Here are some examples of fixed versus growth mindset traits to get you thinking about your own.

FIXED MINDSET BEHAVIOUR:

- Avoids challenges
- Refuses to receive feedback
- Feels threatened by people who are more successful
- Spirals from mistakes
- Shies away from unfamiliar experiences
- Believes talent is static
- Remains rigid in work processes

GROWTH MINDSET BEHAVIOUR:
- Embraces feedback
- Feels inspired by others' success
- Believes in abundant opportunities
- Learns from mistakes
- Regularly steps outside their comfort zone
- Open to new ways of thinking and operating

You can change the residents in your mind if you do the work. For many people, behaviour can be tricky to change and often requires the help of a professional. Consider working with a coach or therapist to assist you in developing your coping skills for mental fitness – you will live a much more enjoyable life – trust me, it's worth it.

The best way to own your own personal brand is to live intentionally. You will find that if you can look after yourself, you will start to think more clearly, even when life continues to hit you with ongoing ups and downs. Even among all the painful stuff we go through, human connection and love have the power to steer us through.

By reflecting on your inner world and how it shows up in your relationships, you've started to carry your briefcase with grace and confidence. You're not just talking about your brand – you're living it. Whether it's through honest partnerships, thoughtful advocacy, or a shift in how you speak to yourself, your personal brand is now something you own.

In the next chapter, we'll bring this presence into the digital world, where intention and visibility meet. Because how you show up online is just an extension of how you show up in life. Ready to be seen?

CHAPTER SUMMARY

- **Partnerships are powerful:** WOM marketing can cut through the noise and help curate opportunities and lives you actually want to be part of. Are your partners helping you create the opportunities you desire?

- **Audit your environment:** How is your circle around you? Are you inspired or joyous with the people in your community?

- **Mindset check:** Are you aware of who is residing in your mind? What is your natural default setting?

REFLECTION QUESTIONS

- How do your current partnerships – personal and professional – support or challenge your personal brand?

- What habits or mindsets are helping or hindering your ability to show up with confidence and clarity?

- What one action can you take today to strengthen the way you present yourself to the world?

CHAPTER 4

AMPLIFY

Social media is not just a trend; it's the way
our society communicates. Your business
needs to be a part of that conversation.

RICHARD BRANSON
founder of Virgin Group

TIMES HAVE CHANGED. There was a time when paying
for media required agencies and a significant budget.
Today, in an internet-first society, social media platforms
have become accessible to everyone, providing the ability,
agency and choice to reach a global audience and pursue
our dreams.

In the past, opportunities were limited by who we knew.
Our identities were shaped by the resources available to us –
geographically, socially and economically. Now the internet
allows us to connect with a much wider audience. While this
shift has both positive and negative impacts, it's essential to
recognise its significance.

We no longer need to wait to be noticed by our local
community or employer. The digital world has erased bor-
ders, allowing us to curate our own stories, build trust and
share expertise on our terms. Social media often serves

as the first point of contact, sometimes even before professional relationships are established. We can't afford to underestimate its impact. Even if you don't meet someone through LinkedIn, chances are you'll look them up online to assess their credibility and worldview before deciding whether to meet, work or collaborate with them.

If you're new to social media, know that I only started posting more frequently on my personal accounts in 2016. My professional presence on LinkedIn began just two and a half years ago when I entered the startup tech world, initially to promote my company's work. Before that, I had no branding or professional online presence. I was the type of person who went to work, did a great job, went home, and spent time with family and friends – no networking, no presence, nothing.

My career progression relied entirely on the managers and leaders around me (which was frustrating). When I relocated to Sydney in 2018, I was contacted via LinkedIn for an interview with a global strategy firm. Even though I had minimal presence, I had done just enough to be found on their scouting systems. Looking back, I can only imagine what opportunities I might have unlocked if I had invested in this sooner. This is a common mistake I see – people only start building their online presence when they're actively seeking their next job. Don't make that mistake.

I recently learned in a businesswoman group session that it used to take six points of contact to build trust. With the overwhelming amount of content and the rise of generative AI, trust now requires closer to twelve points of contact. People want to see consistency before they engage. With this in mind, the online world is waiting to be harnessed.

Of course, social media has its downsides. Many platforms are designed to capture your attention, and exploring your relationship with them is important. However, if you want to build an impactful and consistent personal brand, some online presence helps – both now and in the future. The key is to do it in a way that aligns with who you are, and being online is not a matter of life or death; I know lots of people who don't engage in any of it because they don't want to. If that's you, then that is completely okay. But we are moving towards becoming more digital as a society, and branding online might not be as bad as you think!

In this chapter, we'll explore a few things:

- The stories of individuals who have leveraged their online presence to build strong personal brands.

- We'll also address common myths – that you need to be perfect, widely known, or have a loud personality to make an impact online.

- The goal of this chapter is to give you the tools and confidence to grow your business and pursue your goals.

The power of online branding in a noisy market

At a recent panel discussion on building and scaling tech teams, a recurring challenge stood out – hiring and opening doors is significantly harder without a strong company brand. Building a company's brand takes time; a logo or catchy tagline is no longer enough. People still seek genuine connections in an era of information overload and growing distrust. After the event, I posted on my channels about how personal branding can be a powerful competitive advantage in today's crowded market. Here are some of the key points:

- **CEO reputation matters**. A study conducted by Weber Shandwick in collaboration with KRC Research surveyed over 1,700 executives across nineteen countries. They found executives worldwide attribute 44% of their company's market value and nearly half (45%) of a company's reputation to the CEO's personal reputation.[30]

- **People buy from people.** As Grace Gong (top LinkedIn and Silicon Valley voice for venture capital) put it so well, we live in an internet-first era where your online presence serves as social proof, both professionally and personally. Leila Oliveira (top LinkedIn leading voice in venture capital) shared that due diligence on founders often starts online. I also know that many executive search professionals rely on LinkedIn when evaluating candidates, and many news stories are sourced from online social media platforms.

- **Social media influence drives business.** LinkedIn's insights team shared at SXSW last year (2024) that 56% of professionals say a business executive's presence on social media positively influences their purchase decision, while 68% are more likely to recommend a company or brand if they follow an executive online.

- **Employees have greater reach than corporate accounts.** Brand messages gain more traction when shared through employees' personal accounts rather than the company's official page. The rise of user-generated content (have you seen the marketing lately?) proves that people trust individuals more than brands, especially as a way to cut through noise – consumers are seeking relatability over perfection.

---

30 Weber Shandwick & KRC Research. *The CEO Reputation Premium: Gaining Advantage in the Engagement Era.* 2023.

- **Thought leadership shapes perception**. A strong personal brand can significantly improve potential employees' perception of a company, making it more attractive to top talent. It is also a great inexpensive strategy if you are looking to expand your operations and don't have a large marketing budget – people buy and work for people, your personal brand can be your competitive advantage in a crowded market. I have seen several companies successfully harness their CEO personal brand as part of their expansion.

- **The creator economy is evolving**. The focus is shifting from public fame and content overload to private access and hyper-personalisation. High-paid creators and sought-after professionals are no longer playing the content game, they are monetising access and connection. This means you don't need a massive following to achieve your goals. (Great insight from Doone Roisin, founder of Female Startup Club.)

- **A loyal community fuels business growth**. When companies genuinely invest in a brand, scaling becomes a collaborative effort between the business and its customers. Imagine if customers are advocating your company to your target audience.

- **Storytelling is a competitive edge**. Connection, authenticity and trust are the foundation of modern branding. A compelling story that resonates with your audience will set you apart.

Your personal brand is a key driver of growth and revenue. Investing in online branding is a great avenue to cut through the noise, save costs and attract the right culture, partnerships and talent both locally and globally (if that's on your agenda).

How social media is a game-changer

The internet has transformed how people find opportunities, launch careers and achieve success. While social media has been a powerful tool for celebrities, it's also changing the lives of everyday people.

Social media has made people famous: Justin Bieber was discovered on YouTube at twelve years old; Calvin Harris was discovered on Myspace; and Billie Eilish was discovered on SoundCloud at the age of thirteen when a song meant for her dance teacher went viral. It has also led to people finding work. After a twenty-six-year-old woman genuinely shared her work struggles on TikTok, her video attracted twenty-three million views and a week later she landed her dream job.

These stories highlight how social media is more than just entertainment – it's a tool that could change your life. Whether you're an aspiring artist, a job seeker or an entrepreneur, the internet provides opportunities to showcase your talent, connect with the right people and take control of your future. There is a reason why we are seeing content creation as a career choice!

Storytelling – from ancient to modern

Online content allows us to amplify our presence, knowledge and impact on the world. It is a doorway for people with big ambitions to share their message in the absence of connections; it provides an avenue for those with quieter personalities; and a global platform for people living in remote or rural places, or even on the other side of the world.

Content has also changed over time, but the reason why we are drawn to it hasn't; it has merely evolved. Stories have been shared among tribes from all over the world since the beginning of time. For example:

- **Storytelling fire circles**: Many Indigenous cultures around the world, including Native American, African and Australian Aboriginal communities, held storytelling circles around a fire (e.g., yarn circles for First Nations).

- **Polynesian storytelling circles**: (Hawai'i, Tahiti, Sāmoa, Tonga, Aotearoa) passed down knowledge through *mo'olelo* (stories), *ka'ao* (mythical tales) and *'ōlelo no'eau* (proverbs), song, dance and art – storytelling was embodied, not just spoken.

- **Hindu Sabha gatherings**: In ancient India, *sabhas* (community assemblies) hosted *kathakas* – storytellers who recited epic tales like the *Ramayana* and *Mahabharata* in temple courtyards and village squares.

- **Norse mead halls (Viking culture)**: The Vikings gathered in mead halls, such as the legendary Heorot from *Beowulf*, where skalds (poets) recited sagas and heroic tales of gods and warriors.

- **Mesopotamian storytelling circles (Sumer, Akkad, Babylon, Assyria)**: Storytellers, priests and scholars shared myths in temple schools (*Edubba*), where scribes trained in writing and storytelling, and travellers shared in marketplaces and inns.

I can go on and on across the different empires. Still, you see there is a commonality: stories were shared to preserve knowledge and bring people together, usually by elders or people in the community who held special roles and stories were shared in community spaces. Now imagine the internet is one big community hall, where anyone is able to speak, and you can choose which hall you walk into. We connect through stories. But now it's no longer restricted to geography, gender, age, status or religion – it's open.

I am not excusing the awful part of social media, but story-sharing is part of being human. Sharing your story in your circles is a great tool to get support and build a life that you want to live by growing social connections.

How to tell your story well

People love down-to-earth, relatable content, and we are seeing a trend towards short-form video content. Why are phone calls and in-person interactions so much more impactful than email and text? One reason is that sound is the second sense we develop in our mother's womb, following touch. Auditory development begins at eighteen weeks, and by approximately twenty-four weeks the foetus can respond to external sounds.[31, 32]

The brain processes sound ten times faster than vision (about 0.05 seconds for sound vs 0.5 seconds for vision).

How fast your brain processes sound and visuals matters more than you think

Why does this matter for social media? In a world full of distractions, the faster your message can get through, the better. Sound and visuals grab attention quickly, especially when it comes to video content. Your brain can process video and audio together in a way that grabs immediate focus, unlike text, which takes longer to interpret.

Recent studies show that auditory signals trigger faster brain responses than visuals,[33] meaning videos with sound

---

31 American Academy of Pediatrics. (2012). *Fetal Development and Hearing*. Pediatrics. https://pediatrics.aappublications.org/content/early/2012/05/17/peds.2012-0850.

32 Healthline. (2022, March 1). *When can a fetus hear? Womb development timeline*. Healthline. https://www.healthline.com/health/pregnancy/when-can-a-fetus-hear.

33 Fallon, J., & Pylkkänen, L. (2024). How our brains grasp linguistic structure from parallel visual input. *Science Advances, 10*(43), eadr9951. https://doi.org/10.1126/sciadv.adr9951.

are much more likely to make an impact. Utilising platforms such as Instagram, TikTok or YouTube (and now even LinkedIn), videos that combine engaging visuals and clear audio can get your message across faster and with more emotion than text alone. Without sound or visuals, messages can feel flat or be easily ignored.

Tone speaks louder than words

How something is said – the tone, rhythm or pitch – matters more than the actual words. We can actually hear feelings in voices. It's what makes sarcasm, joy or concern come through clearly, even without seeing a face. Have you experienced this? Studies show that voices convey warmth and emotion better than text.[34] It's how you know someone's joking, or when something's not quite right, even without seeing their expression.

We trust voices more than words on a screen

When we hear someone speak, it builds connection and trust faster than reading a message. This is why podcasts, audiobooks and radio have such loyal listeners – the voice feels human. Recent research revealed that people rate voice-based communication as more persuasive and credible than text-only formats.[35]

---

34 Lu, X., Ho, H. T., Sun, Y., Johnson, B. W., & Thompson, W. F. (2016). The influence of visual information on auditory processing in individuals with congenital amusia: An ERP study. *NeuroImage, 135*, 142–151. https://doi.org/10.1016/j.neuroimage.2016.04.043.

35 Hülsdünker, T., Riedel, D., Käsbauer, H., Ruhnow, D., & Mierau, A. (2021). *Auditory information accelerates the visuomotor reaction speed of elite badminton players in multisensory environments. Frontiers in Human Neuroscience, 15*, 779343. https://doi.org/10.3389/fnhum.2021.779343.

What is your medium of choice?

In today's digital world, building a personal brand isn't just about choosing one platform – it's using multiple channels to connect with different audiences. Each social media platform serves a unique purpose and attracts a distinct audience, making it crucial to tailor your content accordingly.

For example, LinkedIn is a professional space where you can showcase industry insights, career achievements and thought leadership, while Instagram and Tik Tok allow for a more personal, visual and creative expression.

I am transitioning from a purely personal Instagram to a more professional blend that helps bridge the gap between work and personal life, bringing professional connections into a more relatable and engaging environment. The ability to repurpose and cross-share content across platforms – whether from LinkedIn to Instagram, Tik Tok or even WhatsApp stories – ensures that your brand reaches the right people in the right spaces.

I also speak at quite a few events, engage in interviews, and appear on podcasts and YouTube, which provides another platform for people to engage and understand how I operate; this is another powerful way to connect with your audience.

Understanding that different people engage with different platforms is key to effective brand growth. Some audiences prefer professional networking on LinkedIn, while others might connect better through the casual and direct nature of Instagram, Tik Tok or WhatsApp stories.

There are people who avoid social media altogether and those who are selective about the platforms they use. This is why it's important to diversify your content strategy – sharing thought leadership on LinkedIn, (I share now on Tik Tok too), personal yet curated insights on Instagram, and updates on WhatsApp stories for those in your closer circles. By doing so, you meet your audience where they are while maintaining authenticity and control over how much of your brand is visible on each platform.

EXERCISE
GET STARTED
ON SOCIAL MEDIA

If you're reading this book and in the professional space, you're likely considering LinkedIn as one of your platforms. How you choose to integrate your personal and professional content is up to you. When I work with clients, I usually ask the following questions to help guide the process:

- What kind of content excites you? What do you like to listen to? Why?

- What kind of content drains or repulses you?

- Does anyone's online or offline presence inspire you? Why?

- What mediums do you prefer engaging with – podcasts, videos, or written word?

- Do you have a question to help you filter whether you should post content?

Here are a few ways to get started with creating content, no matter what space you are in:

- **Storytelling**: Share your story, an interesting insight or something fun. I usually share insights from a conference or event that I find interesting (chances are, someone else will).

- **Problem-solving**: Highlight a problem (common or specific) and share solutions that will resonate with your target audience (make sure this is aligned with your offerings).

- **Mistakes:** Discuss common mistakes people make in your domain, creating a sense of urgency and establishing authority in the space.

- **Funny/wholesome:** People enjoy content that brings people together or makes them smile, and it helps with positive association. One of my more popular videos was taken at my friends' weddings when I wearing a sari and showing what was in the briefcase, piece by piece.

TIPS AND TRICKS TO HELP YOU GET STARTED

- Everything you put online is a digital tattoo. Ask yourself this before you post anything: Is this something I'm comfortable sharing with my current and future employers/clients/partners?

- Cut through the noise by posting something useful and aligned with you; people are here to learn about you.

- Start posting, don't wait until it's perfect!

- Reply to comments, use hashtags, and tag people and their companies whenever you can.

- Keep self-promotion and thought leadership separate; people don't enjoy being sold to. Use social media as a tool to build your credibility and authority.

You can use other methods to increase your sales if that's part of your goals. As we partner more with machine learning, please remember to relay your experience and expertise in a way that's accessible to humans, but straightforward enough for a machine to interpret. Remember to use hand gestures! According to a study by Vanessa van Edwards, who analysed numerous *TED Talks*, the most popular speakers used an average of 465 hand gestures in eighteen minutes, while the least popular used only 272.[36]

Social media is simply an evolution of how we share stories. We are wired to learn with stories, and they are the magic, whether you consume them via books, podcasts, movies or TV shows, that help us connect more with humanity. No matter what platform you choose to engage on, it's important to understand the power of storytelling for your personal brand; online connections could provide the path towards your next great opportunity.

You don't need to go viral to be valuable. A strong digital presence isn't about numbers – it's about resonance. When people see your content, your tone and your values, do they feel something? That's personal branding at its best.

In a time when attention is currency, your story is your asset. When you lead with clarity and consistency, opportunities find you. Not because you shouted the loudest, but because you stood out for being real.

'Someday is not a day of the week.'

JANET DAILEY
author

---

36 Van Edwards, V. (n.d.). *20 hand gestures you should be using*. Medium. Retrieved from https://medium.com/@vvanedwards/20-hand-gestures-you-should-be-using-c8717eca02d7.

You've done the work: unpacked your briefcase, arranged it with care, walked it with confidence, and now it's time for you to share it with the world. There's only one thing left to do – keep showing up.

CHAPTER SUMMARY

- **Storytelling sticks:** From ancient history to social media. We are wired to learn through storytelling, so remember the way we engage has changed over time, but the reason we are drawn to stories has remained the same since our ancestors first began telling stories.

- **The digital world is a game-changer:** Social media has removed traditional barriers, allowing individuals to build their brands, connect with a global audience and create opportunities on their own terms.

- **Authenticity matters more than ever.** The online space is noisy, but trust is built through consistency and authenticity. People resonate with real stories, not just polished marketing.

- **Your online presence is a digital tattoo.** Everything you post contributes to your personal brand. Being intentional about your digital footprint can open doors to career growth, business opportunities and meaningful connections.

REFLECTION QUESTIONS

- How does your current online presence reflect your personal brand and values?

- What kind of content do you naturally engage with, and how can you create similar content that feels authentic to you?

- Is there a preferred social medium you like to engage with?

- What fears or limiting beliefs hold you back from putting yourself out there online?

CONCLUSION

I F YOU'VE MADE it this far, you're already in rare air. Less than one per cent of people give themselves the permission to pause, reflect and choose who they want to become (recognising that so much of this world does not get this privilege).[37] So, thank you – for backing yourself. Your essence will naturally curate a life where love for humanity is stronger than any need to exploit from it. Imagine how much brighter and more beautiful the world will be with your presence.

The Briefcase Effect was never about ticking societal boxes or curating a performance. It was always about helping you align what you say, think and do so you can build a life you enjoy, not because of your success or status but regardless of them. You don't need a perfect life to be powerful. Resonance lives in consistency. When your voice, tone and ideas are aligned – people feel it. That's presence

I hope by now you're beginning to see that everything you need has been with you all along. The Briefcase Effect isn't about becoming someone else, but about peeling back the noise and insecurities and elevating your environment

---

37 According to the people I have met invested in this book – wow! Elite!

so you can show up with courage and take aligned action, even when it's messy.

You now have the power to take ownership of your story, your desires, your dreams and your part in making the world better than when you arrived. You're ready to commercialise your natural gifts and design a personal brand, through the pursuit of mastery framework, that reflects the real you, not a curated version.

Your personal brand is not built in isolation. We're not meant to do this alone. From the beginning of time, humans have connected through shared stories, mutual care and a deep need to belong. Unlike most other species, humans have the longest vulnerability period in early life.

That hasn't changed. Social media is a commercial evolution of a campfire. Invest in people. Invest in community. Share what's in your briefcase and listen to what's in theirs. You never know which part of your story will open a door for someone else.

So, what now?

Find your own briefcase – it may turn up in the most unexpected place, as mine did – then see what is inside and curate what you want to carry, leave behind and amplify. No matter where you go, it comes and evolves with you, so if you ever feel lost, return to this book's questions and exercises. Among all the chaos, always remember to have fun with this crazy thing called life!

LET'S CONNECT

I F YOU'VE REACHED the end of this book – thank you! I am quite active and vocal on my socials, and if you are interested in thought leadership and witnessing the raw unfiltered spectrum of the human experience, I'd love to stay connected. You can find me:

- **LinkedIn**: Vinisha Rathod (look for the fairy and the briefcase)
- **Instagram**: @vinii_shar
- **TikTok**: @vini.sha_p3studio
- **Website**: www.thebriefcaseeffect.com
- **Email**: vinisha@p3studio.com.au

If you would like more information, check out my website or see below. I work with individuals, organisations and communities – whether you're scaling a team, navigating a transition or simply figuring out your next move.

Personal Brand Strategy

For individuals and teams

My signature personal brand intensives are available one on one or in group formats. These are deep, collaborative sessions designed to help you articulate your value, build your blueprint and step up with confidence.

Keynote Speaking & Facilitation

For conferences, offsites and leadership programs

I speak and facilitate on topics such as authenticity, diversity, personal branding, early or mid-careers, and navigating identity in complex spaces. My sessions are equal parts practical, playful and powerful and create safe spaces that welcome nuance and action.

Business Partnering

For founders, executives, teams and growing businesses

I partner with growing organisations to align people, purpose and performance. From startup to enterprise, I bring structure, clarity and culture strategy to help you become aligned, profitable and a great place to work.

ACKNOWLEDGEMENTS

To my incredible family and friends who continually encouraged me, and to all of you who were not even surprised that I was writing a book.

To my grandmas, Mum and every ancestor who ever fought so I am able to be given the opportunity to build a career and life on my terms, thank you from the bottom of my heart. Thank you for all the fighting so my essence and I could truly partner with the world; your efforts will not be wasted.

To my dad for teaching me everything that I know: thank you for teaching me critical thinking, and to never take anyone or any life for granted. Thank you for leaving behind the most beautiful family that I get to share both my highs and lows with.

To my late grandfathers for all their love and for believing in me, I so appreciate how loved and adored I was. I hope you can see your tenacity, love for humanity and entrepreneurship flowing in everything I do.

To my life and business coaches, therapist, acupuncturist, doctors, trainers and the service professionals who I've worked with, thank you for everything you do.

To my friend Laetitia, who inspired me to write this book. When I shared that I was on the precipice of something big, she said that I must write a book! She connected me with Scott at Grammar Factory; the rest is history.

Thank you to the team at Grammar Factory. It takes a village to raise a child, an army for a business and an elite team to help polish a book that has the power to help every single person live to their full potential.

To every person who believed in me, to the Australian tech community which welcomed me with open arms, to every one of you who are listening, reading, purchasing, sharing and delighting me with your warmth, ears and eyes. Thank you for spending your moments with me, and thank you for taking the step to wear your essence on your sleeve. Imagine how much brighter and more beautiful the world will be with your presence.

I would also like to mention how much I enjoy any cuisine that has leek in it. I see you, Leek, and I am here for your delightful value.

ABOUT THE
AUTHOR

VINISHA RATHOD is an author, keynote speaker, and Managing Director of P3 Studio.

With over fifteen years of experience across government, tech, corporates and not-for-profits, she's the go-to partner for leadership, strategy and culture that works in the real world.

Often called the Startup Fairy for her refreshing authenticity and sharp insights, Vinisha works with founders, investors and operators to cut through the noise. Whether it's uplifting your culture and teams, redesigning your organisation, or dealing with the human messiness of growing companies, Vinisha brings both commercial acumen and empathy to the room.

The Briefcase Effect is based on her signature one-on-one and workshops. This book is a practical deep-dive for anyone seeking alignment, agency and traction.

As a fierce advocate for systems that reward merit and capability, she's driven by a bigger mission: breaking glass ceilings and ending domestic violence through economic empowerment and community.

May your love for humanity be stronger than your need to exploit from it.

If you're building or seeking, she'd love to hear from you.

www.ingramcontent.com/pod-product-compliance
Lightning Source LLC
Chambersburg PA
CBHW022113210326
41597CB00047B/461